FOLLOW YOUR DREAMS

MYCHAL WYNN

MYCHAL WYNN

FOLLOW
YOUR
DREAMS

RISING SUN
PUBLISHING

FOLLOW YOUR DREAMS

Second Edition, 2007

Follow Your Dreams: *Lessons That I Learned in School*
Printing 1 2 3 4 5 6

Library of Congress Control Number: 2001088883

ISBN-13: 978-1-880463-51-2

ISBN-10: 1-880463-51-2

Reference sources for style and usage: *The New York Public Library
Writer's Guide to Style and Usage* copyright 1994 by The New
York Public Library and the Stonesong Press, Inc., and the *APA
Stylebook 2004* by the Associated Press.

The poems, *Dare, If You Are My Friend,* and *There's A New Day
Coming*, are reprinted from the book, *Don't Quit – Inspirational
Poetry.*

RISING SUN
PUBLISHING
P.O. Box 70906
Marietta, Georgia 30007-0906
800.524.2813
info@rspublishing.com
web site: http://www.rspublishing.com

Printed in the United States of America.

Acknowledgments

I would like to thank my parents who protected, nurtured, and guided me along the journey to discovering my dreams; Mrs. Burke, my kindergarten teacher; Mr. Roberts, my fifth- and sixth-grade teacher; Dr. Cheryl R. Gholar, my high school Job Placement Counselor; Dean Roland Latham, Dean of Students at Northeastern University; Ernestine Whiting, Director of Financial Aid; Harvette Emmett, my friend and mentor; and to all those who have prayed, supported, and encouraged me to pursue my dreams.

I would also like to thank my editor, Denise Mitchell Smith, my proofreader, Laurie Lowe Sorrells, and my graphic artist, Jennifer Gibbs.

Dedication

This book is dedicated to my wife, Nina, who has stood by me and supported my dreams and the dreams of our children; to my sons, Mychal-David and Jalani; and, to all of the students who have asked me to share the story of how I discovered my dreams.

Contents

Introduction

For over 25 years I have worked with school boards, superintendents, state departments of education, parents, teachers, administrators, and students throughout the United States. My work has taken me beyond America's borders to Canada, Mexico, the Caribbean, Bermuda, and Africa. I have received proclamations from Governors, Keys to Cities, been recognized by the United States Congress, and received plaques and awards from numerous school districts, churches, and community organizations. I have written twenty books (and still writing) that are considered to be some of the most insightful, inspiring, and enlightening. The poems in my book of poetry, *Don't Quit*, have been recited by students at graduation ceremonies and in oratorical contests. My story, *The Eagles who Thought They were Chickens*, has been told and retold by teachers, ministers, motivational speakers, and storytellers. My book, *Ten Steps to Helping Your Child Succeed in School*, has forever changed the lives of parents and their children as they have worked together to discover their dreams.

I have shared my thoughts and ideas with superintendents, school boards, teachers, administrators, government officials, business leaders, and parents about how to create schools of excellence. And, I have talked to over five hundred thousand students about discovering their dreams and aspirations.

In the midst of it all, I have been so busy working to turn schools into places of passion and purpose that I have never taken the time to write about how my passions (writing and talking) developed into my purpose (helping to create great schools) and my career (writing and speaking).

Despite being born poor and having my second grade teacher predict that I would never make it out of elementary school, I am living my dreams. After growing up in an apartment, amidst the gangs and violence of Chicago's South Side, just a stone's throw away from the projects, I now own homes in California, Georgia, and Florida. After being given up for adoption, I now have a loving wife and two handsome and intelligent sons. And, despite the frustration of never being able to find a summer job while growing up in Chicago, my wife and I own our own business and have worked for ourselves for over twenty years.

Many students have asked, "Mr. Wynn, are you rich?" If being rich is measured by how many people respect, admire, like or love you, (as it should be) then, yes, I am rich. I have the best job in the world ... *I am doing what I love to do and I get paid for doing it.* I have my faith, my family, and my health. I am rich beyond measure.

I am sharing my story because I want to inspire you to discover your dreams; work toward your dreams; set goals to guide your efforts toward achieving your dreams; and, I want you to live your dreams so you, too, may live a rich life.

Perhaps one day you will share your story with others and inspire them to discover their dreams.

DARE

Dare to be different
    when all around you seek conformity

Dare to encounter obstacles
    when all around you avoid conflict

Dare to seek possibilities
    when all around you see only the impossible

Dare to seek new and greater challenges
    when all around you are procrastinating

Dare to remain strong
    when all around you are weakening

Dare to continue
    when all around you are quitting

Dare to have faith
    when all around you are doubting

Dare to dream
    even if no one dreams with you

— Mychal Wynn

Chapter 1

In the Beginning

When I was born, there was nothing to suggest that I would have any great dreams or achieve anything extraordinary in my life. I was not born rich. I was not born brilliant. I was not born with an extraordinarily high I.Q. My parents were not doctors, lawyers, politicians, teachers or business owners. In fact, they were not even married. My father was not a publisher and my mother was not a writer. They did not have plans to send me to a private school. I was not born into a big house. We did not have a butler, a maid, a chauffeur or even a car.

When I was born, surviving was the most important thing. Getting a job as a sharecropper or picking cotton, working as a dishwasher, waitress or seamstress, maybe, but to dream of becoming a writer—NOT. At least, not where I was born.

I was born to a single mother (which means that she was not married to my father) who already had one son. She was very poor and lived in one of the poorest parts of the country (rural Alabama). I was not born in a hospital, I was born in a "shotgun shack." They were called shotgun shacks because you could walk into the front door, take five to ten steps, and walk straight out of the back door. They had "outhouses," which means that the toilets were outside of the houses. They were little wooden sheds with a hole in the ground! Times were tough and the people were poor.

I do not know how old my mother was, what she looked liked, what she believed or if she even loved me. All that I know is what my court records state and what people have told me.

My court records state that I was born in Pike County, Alabama, on July 7, 1956. Pike County is a poor rural county about 40 miles from Montgomery, Alabama. Although 1956 was not really that long ago, to most of the students whom I speak to in schools today, it may as well have been a hundred years ago. Even when I talk with my own children about where I was born, they look at me like there could not have been any place like that on earth; and certainly not in the United States. They cannot imagine living in a house where you have to get up and go outside to use the bathroom or living in a house that does not have running water, a shower or a bathtub.

The year, 1956, was a significant time in the history of the United States. A few months earlier, Rosa Parks, a black woman, had refused to give up her seat on a bus in Montgomery, Alabama, to a white man (which was against the law at that time). Most of the students I talk to cannot imagine that either. While many young people today choose to sit in the back of the bus, when I was born, the law stated that black people *had* to sit in the back of the bus and that they *had* to stand up and give their seats to white people.

Well, Mrs. Parks had been working hard all day as a seamstress and dreamed of resting her tired, aching body, and getting off of her tired, aching feet. She just wanted to sit down in one of those bus seats for her ride home. Unfortunately, few people cared about the dreams of black people or other minorities, whether they were Native American, Hispanic, Asian or women. In fact, many laws were written to keep people from dreaming of getting the education that they needed to follow their dreams; dreams of good jobs; dreams of eating wherever they wanted to eat; dreams of going wherever they wanted to go; dreams of living wherever they wanted to live; or dreams of taking a ride on the bus and just being left alone! Rosa Parks was a hardworking, tired black woman who only dreamed of resting her tired, aching feet by sitting on one of those bus seats (which were not even comfortable) and she was not allowed even that simple dream!

When the bus seats were filled, the bus driver told Mrs. Parks to get up and give her seat to a white man. I do not know if it was because Mrs. Parks was tired, angry, or both, but she refused to give up her seat. Rosa Parks reminds me of my wife, Nina. Most of the time, she is an easy-going person, and will do anything for her family and friends. However, there are days when people can wear on her nerves and she just says, "Enough is enough!" Those are the days when everyone should duck. When she has had enough, she is not going to take any more. On those days, my boys and I usually go to the park, take a walk, go to the movies or anything. We just know to leave her alone. Well, this was one of those days for Rosa Parks. I can imagine that she said to herself, "Enough is enough. My feet are tired and I ain't going to move."

Rosa Parks was sent to jail because she would not give up her seat. That eventually led to the Montgomery Bus Boycott and the beginning of what became known as the Civil Rights Movement. It could even be called the "Dream Movement."

Much of what people in America have the freedom to do today, particularly women and people of color, has resulted from the dreams of millions of people during that time in our country's history. People who dreamed of the freedom to vote; dreamed of the freedom to eat wherever they chose; dreamed of living wherever they chose and of buying a house wherever they could afford to live; dreamed of the freedom to attend whatever school they chose; dreamed of the freedom to drink from any public water fountain, to use any public rest room or to sit in whatever bus seat they chose. And, people who dreamed of the right to equally pursue the American Dream.

The year that I was born, 1956, may be considered the year that millions of dreams were born throughout America. Maybe my mother gave me up for adoption because she had a dream that another family would help me escape the poverty of Pike County, Alabama. Since I have never met or spoken to my biological mother, I do not know what she actually thought. What I do know is that as an undernourished, crying, dirty little baby, I was given up for adoption when I was six months old.

In 1956, the year of the Montgomery Bus Boycott, I was put on a segregated bus and sent northward from Montgomery, Alabama, to Sharon, Pennsylvania. It was in Sharon, Pennsylvania, that my biological father's aunt arranged to have me adopted by her best friend, who lived in Chicago, Illinois.

Where you come from does not determine where you are going, only where you began.

CHAPTER 2

Growing Up Poor

Peple talk a lot about poor children. They feel sorry for them and assume that they are stupid. I know a lot about poor. I was born poor, I grew up poor, I went to college poor, and I began my first job out of college, poor. My biological mother was poor. My adoptive parents were poor. Most of my relatives and all of the people I grew up with were poor. Yes, I know a lot about being poor.

If you are poor or if you know someone who is poor, I have this advice for you, "Poor is a financial condition. Do not allow it become your mental condition!" My mother always told me, "Mychal, don't ever say that you're poor. Just say that you don't have any money." She always taught me that words have power and that if you say that you are poor, then you will put poverty into your consciousness. However, if you say that you are rich—in your health, in your spirit, and in your intelligence—then you will be putting wealth into your consciousness. If you put wealth into your consciousness, one day it will make its way into your pocket. My mother was right. There have been lots of times in my life when I did not have any money. However, I never thought of myself as poor. Broke, maybe; without money, certainly; but poor, never. My consciousness was a wealth consciousness, which was permanent. My financial condition—not having any money— was a temporary condition.

I go to a lot of schools where I hear students who come from poor families (like where I came from) making excuses, "Why should I work hard? Nobody is going to give me a job" or "I'm going to be a basketball player so I don't have to study" or worse "I can't learn this." I hear students who speak like I did, using broken English, non-standard grammar, profanity or slang, and who will not speak Standard English (correct grammar according to the rules of the English language) because they say that it is "talking white!" I also hear students saying, "I don't want to get good grades because I don't want to act white." After growing up poor, I can tell you this: Knowing the rules of grammar, working hard, and getting good grades has nothing to do with acting "white!" It has to do with acting like you are tired of being poor and with wanting to do something about it. Learning how to speak will get you a good job. Learning how to think will get you a good job. And, in case you did not know it, doing well in school will provide you with the opportunity to not only get a good job but to create your own job by starting your own business. I also hear students complaining, "My teacher doesn't like me" or "This work is too hard and nobody helps me." While it may be true that some teachers do not like you, and that some people will not help you, I know for a fact that when people help themselves, there are a lot of people who will be *inspired* to help them. That is an important word, "Inspired." Most of what people achieve in life comes as a result of inspiration and perspiration. Those two words describe how my wife and I built our publishing company—inspiration and perspiration.

When people are working hard to learn, there are a lot of people who will work just as hard to teach them. Their perspiration and hard work inspires people to help them. The simple truth is, people who try, inspire others to help them, while people who complain, inspire others to leave them alone!

You do not have to be a genius to know that there is opportunity everywhere in America. Despite whatever problems or obstacles you face, the fact remains that there is more opportunity in America than perhaps anywhere else on the planet. If you cannot find opportunity in America, then it is because you are spending more time focusing on yesterday's problems than on today's opportunities. And, you are probably spending more time feeling sorry for yourself than researching where the opportunities are.

The window of opportunity is opening and closing, continually, throughout your lifetime. However, each time that the window of opportunity opens, there are a lot of other people trying to go through before it closes. That is called "competition," a fact of life. Take it or leave it, like it or lump it, that is just the way it is. Whether a football game or Spelling Bee, a college application or a job application, a Science Fair or a Track Meet, a cheerleading tryout or a band audition, throughout your lifetime you are going to be confronted with competition for each opportunity. You have a choice. You can prepare yourself for the inevitable competition or you can sit around complaining and feeling sorry for yourself.

I meet a lot of teachers who feel sorry for poor children—I don't. I was poor and I did not need anyone to feel sorry for me. I needed people to help prepare me to compete. I needed people to help me discover the potential that I did not realize I had. I needed people to help me to discover my dreams and to develop a plan of how to achieve those dreams. I needed someone to help me develop my "game."

Most people would not think of going to the basketball court without "game," or preparing for a major track and field meet without game. Tiger Woods is becoming the greatest golfer that ever lived because his "B" game is better than everyone else's and his "A" game may be the best game, ever, in his sport. Michael Jordan retired as one of, if not the best basketball players that ever played in the NBA because his "B" game was better than everyone else's "A" game and his "A" game was the best, ever. Dr. Mae Jemison, who holds degrees in chemical engineering, African-American studies, and medicine needed her "A" game to successfully complete the NASA astronaut training program, allowing her to become the first African-American woman in space in her role as the science-mission specialist aboard the Space Shuttle Endeavour in September, 1992. Dr. Ben Carson led a team of surgeons through a 24-hour operation, successfully separating Siamese Twins joined at the brain. Needless to say, he and his team of surgeons brought their "A" game.

It is the same with school, getting a job, and doing something about your future. You have got to have game! Being smart has nothing to do with acting white. Being smart has to do with taking care of business so that you increase your opportunity to succeed. The greatest obstacle to anyone's success is KNOWLEDGE—plain and simple. Regardless of what color you are, how poor you are, where you were born, where you live, what you look like, whether or not your mama helps you with your homework, whether or not you have a computer at home or whether or not you even have a home to go to, expand your knowledge and you will expand your opportunity. If you know little, then you can achieve little. If you know a lot, then you can achieve a lot. The question is, "You got game?"

A few years ago, I met with nearly 300 students at Washington High School in Los Angeles, California. Each of the students in the assembly had failed one or more classes. Many of the students were on the free lunch program so many of them probably came from poor families like I did. I was talking to them about their dreams and about whether or not their attitudes were consistent with achieving their dreams. One of the young ladies in the room was in the twelfth grade. She had "major attitude." When I asked what her dreams were, she rolled her eyes and said, "I'm gonna be a doctor!" I then asked, "What type of doctor do you want to become?" She put her hands on her hips and responded, "One that get paid!" All of her friends thought that this was funny. I then asked, "Do you want to be an OB/GYN, Pediatrician, Orthopedic Surgeon, Anesthesiologist or Neurologist?" to which she responded, "Yeah, I'm gonna be all of them." Finally, I asked, "What's your plan? When you graduate, this year, from Washington High School, what is going to be your next step toward becoming a doctor?" She rolled her eyes and said, "I'm gonna go down to the County Hospital and fill out one of those doctor applications!"

If she did not have so much attitude, someone may have told her that she was not going to become a doctor by filling out a job application. Someone may have told her that her kindergarten-through-third-grade work had prepared her for her fourth-grade CTBS (Comprehensive Tests of Basic Skills) testing. Her fourth-grade CTBS test scores had determined the advanced classes she qualified for in middle school. Her middle school grades and her seventh-grade test scores had determined the advanced classes (i.e., honors and AP) she qualified for in high school (she had not, in fact, qualified for any advanced classes either in middle school or high school, and, she had failed several of her regular ed classes and was in danger of not graduating). Her high school GPA, SAT/ACT scores, teacher recommendations, discipline infractions, and extracurricular activities had already determined whether or not she had a good chance of being accepted into a college with a pre-medical program. Not having taken her grades, test scores, or attitude seriously, she had already severely limited her options of getting into college, let alone, into medical school. If her dream was truly to become a doctor, it would not require filling out a job application, it would require a major attitude adjustment!

Unless these students were born with a mental deficiency or other birth defect, they were not born stupid. They, like you and me, were born with limitless intellectual capacity. Scientists have theorized that we use less than 12 percent of our total intellectual capacities. People who are using only as much as 15 percent of their total brain power are considered geniuses. There are at least 8 different ways that each person can demonstrate intelligence. A person can be *word smart* (reading and writing); *problem-solving smart* (math, science, computers, organizing things, and figuring things out); *image smart* (art, drawing, interior design, fashion design, and creating things); *people smart* (working well with, and understanding, people); *self smart* (understanding yourself and being spiritually centered); *musically smart* (singing, composing or playing instruments); *body smart* (dance, martial arts, gymnastics, tumbling, jumping rope or sports); or *environmentally smart* (having a special knowledge of, and connection with, the world around you).

This young lady and the rest of the students were not failing because they were stupid or because they were poor, they were failing because they were making bad choices. They chose to come to school each day with a negative attitude. They chose to be disrespectful to their teachers, clown around, and not do their work. Many of them had major attitudes when their teachers asked them to read or to answer questions in class. Their attitudes were, "Why are you calling on me? I don't know any of this stuff. I'm just coming to hang out." They were choosing not to read, write, discuss or develop their thoughts. They were choosing to come to class late, fall asleep, and make excuses. This had nothing to do with being poor. They were making choices and eventually they were going to suffer the consequences. Their problem was not stupidity, it was insanity! The choices that they were making were not going to help them out of poverty. Each day in school for them was another wasted opportunity.

People do not realize that the human brain is a big muscle made up of billions of neurons that are constantly receiving, transferring, and storing information. Each neuron is made up of dendrites that contribute to brain growth throughout an entire lifetime. Whether we are awake or sleeping, our brain is constantly working, growing, and learning. However, like any other muscle in the body we have to exercise and stretch the brain like we stretch and exercise legs, arms or abdominal muscles. When I was growing up, I often behaved like that young lady, but fortunately my insanity stopped, my intellectual capacity expanded, and I discovered my dreams. Unfortunately, for her, she was a senior in high school and sabotaging her opportunity of going to college or ever becoming a doctor. Even if she did become a doctor, would you want her to be your doctor?

Now, let's go back to being poor. Many students come from families who do not have a lot of money. They may be on welfare. They may live with grandparents, older brothers and sisters, aunts and uncles, in foster homes, homeless or in any number of other situations. Unlike I was when I grew up, my children are not poor. However, if our publishing company went bankrupt, they would be poor. It would not be their fault. But they would nevertheless be poor, like I was, and like millions of others throughout America. Anyone can go to bed rich tonight and wake up poor tomorrow. While the change in their financial condition may be outside of their control, how they respond to their circumstances (i.e., their mental condition) is within their control.

If you wanted to be good at basketball would being poor stop you from developing your lay-ups or jump shot? If you wanted to be good at track would being poor stop you from stretching your muscles and running? If you wanted to dance or rap would being poor stop you from developing your raps or practicing your dance steps? While being poor may keep you from buying the most expensive basketball shoes, if you got "game," you can play in any kind of shoes. Being poor may keep you from buying the most expensive track shoes, but in Africa they run barefoot and are among the best runners in the world. The bottom line is that being poor does not keep anyone from learning, but being lazy and having low expectations does!

I speak to you from personal experience. I grew up in a poor community. All of my friends and all of my cousins received food stamps. A lot of people did not have jobs. My friends did not have a lot of clothes and most of them had shoes with holes in them. In fact, all of *my* shoes had holes in them. I stuffed cardboard into the soles of my shoes to cover the holes. My mother sewed patches over the holes in my clothes. In the cold Chicago winters, I wore two T-shirts, three shirts, two sweaters, and two jackets because I could not afford a warm winter coat.

I have never forgotten how people thought that being poor meant that I was stupid. In the schools that I go to today, there are still people who think that poor children are stupid or who feel sorry for poor children. It is people like these who keep poor people in poverty. Instead of inspiring them to dream of a better future, they convince them to stop dreaming. And, when children have the courage to dream, there are people who tell them that their dreams are "unrealistic." I hate that word, "unrealistic." People thought that it was unrealistic for people to fly and then the Wright Brothers proved them wrong. People thought that it was unrealistic for a doctor to perform open-heart surgery and then Dr. Daniel Hale Williams proved them wrong. People thought that space travel was unrealistic and today, space shuttle launches are almost as common as flying from Florida to California. Do not give up on your dreams because they seem difficult or because something has not been done before. Every day someone is opening a new business, discovering a new cure or developing a new idea. Why not you?

One of the books that I have written is entitled, *The Eagles who Thought They were Chickens*. It is about baby eagles that grow up in a chicken yard. The chickens talk about them and call them stupid because they are different. The chickens and roosters put them down and pick on them the way that people put me down and picked on me because I was poor. While two of the eagles learn how to believe in themselves and learn how to fly, one of the eagles allows what the chickens and roosters say about him to convince him that he cannot fly—that he is dumb and ugly. He will not even try. He will live his entire life in the chicken yard. It is like students, who, because they are poor or have difficulty learning, they will not even try. They will live their entire lifetime in poverty with no hope, no dreams, no aspirations, and no future. In the story, the last eagle will not spread his wings. He will not lift his head. He will not try. He allows others (the chickens and roosters) to convince him that he cannot fly. Even when he sees the other two eagles fly away, he still does not believe in himself. That is how it is for many students. They look around at other students getting *A*'s. They see other students doing well, but they keep making excuses and feeling sorry for themselves. Do not allow this to happen to you. Do not allow people to convince you that you cannot succeed and do not convince yourself that you should not try.

Every time I drive through the community where I grew up, I look around and see people standing on the street corners and I think about that story. Someone, somewhere, convinced them that they could not pursue their dreams and their dreams faded into the sunset. They lost their hope and they gave up on life. They are like the eagle who did not believe that he could fly. And, for them, like me, it began all the way back in elementary school when people began to laugh at them or think less of them because they were poor.

If you ever meet a person who believes that "free or reduced lunch" means stupid, tell them that Mr. Wynn was on free lunch and that all that it meant was that he did not have to pay for lunch! And, if you ever hear people making fun of poor children, students in special ed., people with special needs or anyone else, tell them, "It is cowardly to make fun of someone else's situation. It takes courage to help people overcome their situations."

I also have a message to people, particularly students, who are poor. If you choose not to learn to read, if you choose not to learn to write, if you choose not to learn to think for yourself, if you choose not to set goals and pursue your dreams, then you are choosing to stay poor. If you are poor and going to college is expensive, how are you going to go to college? Do your work and earn a scholarship! And, if you are not planning to go to college, think again. Going to college is not an option no more than going to elementary school is. I know that many people become successful without going to college, however, I also know that many more people will spend the rest of their lives living in poverty because they did not go to college. As a father, I expect my sons to go to preschool, elementary school, middle school, high school and college. If they do not want to go to graduate school, law school or medical school, then that is their choice. However, they are both going to college—period!

If you have decided that you are going to college, but that you are going to get an athletic scholarship, that is great. However, what if you break your leg or arm or something else happens to you and you cannot play basketball or football or whatever? What about an academic scholarship? That is the kind of scholarship that you get for working as hard at your schoolwork as you do developing your crossover dribble. And guess what? You are less likely to break your brain than you are to break your leg.

There was only one guy from my high school who made it into the NBA, Maurice Cheeks, who played professional basketball with the Philadelphia 76ers. I did not know anyone else who got an athletic scholarship; made it into professional basketball, football or baseball, or did well enough in school to have a real chance at life. It did not make any sense. They came to school every day and chose not to do the work. They went to classes every day (at least most days) and chose not to read their books or do the assignments. They had great crossover dribbles and awesome dunks, but they could not tell you the capital of the state where they wanted to play basketball and they could not put together a sentence with correct subject/verb agreement.

You may say, "Why are the state capitals or subject/verb agreement important?" My answer to you is, "Because they were taught." Each day in school, there is a wonderful opportunity to exercise your brain in the same way as you exercise your arms and legs. There is an opportunity to expand your knowledge. A lot of what is taught in school may not be important, but why try to decide what will be important and what will not be important? Just learn it all. Most people do not watch TV the way they study. They do not watch a program and try to decide while the program is running what is important and what is not important. They just watch the entire program. Then they remember what is important to them. But guess what? Even the unimportant stuff is stored away in your brain, just in case.

While I cannot speak for the people I grew up with, many of whom are now dead, in prison or standing on street corners wasting their lives away, I can tell you this: When I helped my older son with his homework; when I read stories to my younger son; I realized that a lot of stuff that I did not feel was important when I was in school *is* important now that I am a father. While I was not excited about reading aloud in school, I am thankful that I have been able to read stories to my children, and most importantly, that *I can.*

All of the successful people I know, work hard. All of the lazy people I know, hardly work. In fact, I do not know any successful lazy people. You choose!

CHAPTER 3

60615

60615 was the zip code where I lived in Chicago and I was determined that I was going to get out of that zip code. When people looked at our home address, they looked at our zip code, 60615, and it may as well have said, "POOR!" Like I have said, some people believe that POOR means STUPID. There are areas like this all over the country. In Los Angeles, it is South Central or East LA; in St. Petersburg, it is South St. Pete; in Atlanta, it is Techwood; in North Carolina and Tennessee, it is the children who live in the mountains; in Arizona and New Mexico, it is the children who live on the reservation; and in Chicago, it was the South Side, and in particular, 60615. In each of these places, people think that *where* you live somehow causes you to have a brain defect. They think that your zip code classifies you as stupid.

When I was growing up, it was my passion in life to prove them wrong. Now that I am an adult, it is my passion in life to help others to prove them wrong. I was not stupid and I was determined not to be poor for the rest of my life. However, how I behaved in school was not consistent with where I wanted to go in life. For a long time, I was like the young lady at Washington High School—I was not paying attention. Most of the time, the way that I behaved in school was like most of the students whom I see in schools today. They behave as if they want to be poor for the rest of their lives. While I was not stupid, I behaved like I was stupid most of the time that I was in school.

Here is the advice that I wish that someone would have given me when I was in school and the advice that I give my two sons: Once you learn something, once you gain knowledge, no one can take it away from you. And, eventually in life it is what you KNOW that will determine what you get paid.

It is hard for many people to understand what I have just said. It is because they do not KNOW enough. So, I will say it again: What you KNOW will determine what you get paid! I do not care what you decide to do. If you decide to play football, you probably think that you are getting paid to throw the ball or catch the fall or knock somebody down who has the ball—NOT!

You are getting paid because you KNOW enough to practice. You are getting paid because you KNOW enough to begin playing football in high school or college so that someone who works for an NFL team (i.e., a scout) will suggest to someone who actually has the money (i.e., a team owner) to pay you. How much they pay you will not be because they like you, personally, because they know your mama or because they want to give poor people a chance.

They will pay you because you KNOW how to catch a ball; KNOW how to run the ball; KNOW how to throw a ball; KNOW how to kick a ball; or KNOW how to knock somebody down with the ball! They will also expect you to KNOW how to read the playbook; KNOW how to come to practice on time; KNOW how to follow the rules of the game; and, KNOW how to follow instructions. However, before someone offers to pay you for what you KNOW, you must KNOW what types of things you need to know.

For example, professional athletes sign contracts with a Sports Agent who negotiates their contracts with professional sports teams. What and how they are paid is determined by what the Sports Agent negotiates for them. How do you identify an honest agent? How much should you pay the agent to negotiate your contract? How much money should you ask for up front? How much should be in the form of a performance bonus? How much should be deferred compensation in order to reduce your income taxes? How do you market yourself for endorsement contracts? What type of language and presentation skills do you need to cash in on motivational speaking and commercials? What type of professionals such as insurance agents, accountants, attorneys or financial planners do you need to hire? How to you check references? What types of insurance do you need? If you buy your mama a house, should you put it in her name, your name or in the name of a trust? Should you get a mortgage and invest the difference or should you pay cash? How should you invest your money so that you will be financially successful after your career is over? Will you use your money to purchase a franchise, automobile dealership, insurance agency, health club or invest in another type of business that will grow during your football career and become a solid business by the time you retire? How should you take care of your body so that you will be healthy enough to walk, run, jump, and play with your children after your football career is over?

As if all of this is not enough you should KNOW that all of the money is not yours. You will have to pay federal and state income taxes (unless you live in Texas or Florida). You should KNOW how to negotiate the purchase of a home, car, clothes, furniture, and any number of other things that you are going to spend your money on. You need to KNOW how your knowledge and financial success can be used to benefit others. Will you give money to charity? Will you give money to your church? Will you start a non-profit foundation and use some of your money to build a community center, football field or playground to help others who did not have your opportunity? What will be your post-football career? In other words, what type of job will you get once your football career is over? If it was up to me, all retired athletes would become school teachers so that future aspiring athletes would be inspired to become experts at learning in the same way they become experts at catching and throwing balls.

I meet a lot of students who tell me, "I don't need to know all of that stuff. I will hire smart people to read that stuff for me and invest my money." Well, they have a name for athletes like that—STUPID. And, after their careers are over, they have another name for athletes like that—STUPID and BROKE. You need to KNOW that you KNOW that you KNOW! In the words of my niece, "You'd better wake up and recognize!"

The best way to get out of poverty, the best way to ensure a future for yourself and your family, the way that I got out of Chicago, and the way that my wife and I continue to build our business and pursue our dreams is through LEARNING. It amazes me how many people are afraid to learn. One young lady in a middle school told me, "Mr. Wynn, I don't want to get straight *A's*. I might become too smart and my brain may burst." I told her, "Why don't you get straight *A's* the next grading period and come back and tell me whether or not your brain burst."

Our minds are like sponges. We can soak up all types of knowledge and our brains never stop growing. In fact, while you are reading this book, your brain is growing! Just like we choose what we eat for breakfast, we can choose what we feed our brain. Whether we feed it more reading or more math; more English, Spanish, or French; more science, social studies, or history; more speaking or writing; more singing or sports, your brain is like every other muscle in your body. If you do push-ups everyday, your arms and chest muscles (biceps, triceps, and pectorals) will strengthen and grow. If you run each day, your lungs will expand and your heart will grow stronger. The same is true with our brain. If you read, think, write, and speak, each day you will stretch and develop your brain. In fact, if you do this simple exercise, it will be like cross training your brain: *Read for five minutes. Think about what you have read for five minutes. Write about what you have thought about for five minutes. And, talk about what you have written about for five minutes.* Cross training means doing different exercises for a specific period of time at specific intervals. If you can increase your brain workout by five minutes each week, before the end of the school year you will have stretched your brain into a super muscle. Just as bodybuilders flex their muscles in bodybuilding competitions, you will be able to flex your mental muscles (your brain) each day in class.

The book, *Gifted Hands: The Ben Carson Story*, tells the story of Ben Carson, who was poor and was not the best student in school. In fact, he was considered the dumbest kid in his fourth-grade classroom. However, he got a lot smarter after his mother had him do mental cross training by forcing him to memorize his times tables, read a book every week, write a book report about what he would read, and read to her what he had written in his book report. By the end of fifth grade, he was among the smartest students in his classroom and by the end of sixth grade, he had gone from the bottom to the top of his class. He went on to get academic scholarships to Yale University and to the University of Michigan Medical School. He became the youngest director of Pediatric Neurosurgery in the history of Johns Hopkins Medical Center in Baltimore, Maryland,

and went on to lead a 70-member medical team that separated 7-month-old Siamese twins joined at the brain, the first successful operation of its kind ever. From the dumbest kid in class to one of the smartest people on the planet. What about you?

If we feed our brain new information and stretch our brain by developing thoughts and ideas, our brain will grow. When I was growing up I had a passion for arguing (I still do). What I did not know was that thinking about and debating ideas was causing my brain to grow. I may have grown up poor, but I am rich today. You cannot measure how rich I am by what is in my bank account (although it is considerably more than when I was growing up), but by what is in my mind, what is in my heart, and what is in my spirit.

Never forget: Whatever your dreams are, what you eventually get paid, what type of job you get, what type of opportunities you have, where you can live, and where you can travel will all depend on what you know, and on knowing what to do with what you know!

While you do not get to choose where you begin in life, you get to choose where you aspire to go in life.

CHAPTER 4

A New Beginning ...

My parents both grew up in Memphis, Tennessee. My mother went to school with my father's sister and was a grade behind my father, so he did not pay much attention to her when they were in school together. At the end of the eighth grade, my father dropped out of school and eventually was drafted into the Navy. After serving his time in the Navy, he returned home to discover that there were few jobs and little hope for black men in the South during the 60's. Like many other black people in the South he joined what became known as the "Great Migration." That is when black people left the cotton fields and poverty of the South to pursue jobs in the North. My father headed north in search of a better job and a better life. Together, with other men looking for work, my father rode a freight train from Memphis to Chicago with nothing more than his hopes and his dreams.

After struggling along in various odd jobs in Chicago, my father began working for the United States Postal Service. He did not deliver the mail like most of us are familiar with. He loved to drive trucks. In fact, one of his dreams was to sit behind the steering wheel of an 18-wheeler driving across the country, listening to the Blues, and just chill'n. His favorite song was *Jack, That Cat was Clean.* When he started working for the Postal Service, he realized his dream as he drove those big 18-wheelers, stuffed with mail, across the country for the United States Postal Service.

The little girl whom my father did not pay any attention to in elementary school (who became my mother) also moved to Chicago. Now that she was all grown up, my father discovered that she was now a beautiful young woman and they fell in love and got married.

My mother could not have children, but she had always dreamed of becoming a mother and having a child of her own. She prayed constantly for a child and one day her prayers were answered. She got a telephone call from her best friend (my biological father's aunt) who told her that she knew of a baby that needed to be adopted (me).

My mother told me that when she first saw me, I was the most beautiful little baby that she had ever seen. She said that I had nice, big, fat legs but that I was dirty! My hair was all dirty and matted and I just cried and cried. She said that when she gave me my first bottle, I sucked the bottle dry. She went through two more bottles before I stopped crying and fell asleep in her arms. She washed me, combed my matted hair, and dressed me up in a bright new outfit.

My parents took me back to Chicago, Illinois, where I grew up in an apartment on 51st and Dr. Martin Luther King, Jr. Drive. Although our apartment was in one of the poorest sections of Chicago's South Side, it was across the street from Washington Park and a lifetime from Pike County, Alabama. Chicago, like many American cities, has some of the poorest neighborhoods in America and some of the richest neighborhoods in America.

Oprah Winfrey and Michael Jordan, two of the richest and most famous people in America, live in Chicago. But they do not live on the South Side and they do not live anywhere near where I grew up.

The south side of Chicago is where most black people in Chicago live. Not far from where I grew up were the projects. The Chicago projects were huge buildings. Each building was sixteen floors with ten apartments on each floor and anywhere from five to ten or more people living in each apartment. Just do the math; 800 to 1600 people living in one building, in building after building for over 30 city blocks! All of the people were poor and most of the people had lost sight of their hopes, dreams, and aspirations. No wonder there were so many gangs and so much violence in the projects. While most of the people who lived in the projects had lost their hopes and their dreams, all of my cousins and most of my friends were strong enough and had learned enough to make it out. Like I have said before, being poor does not make you stupid and it does not make your dreams unrealistic. I know people who grew up in the projects who are now principals, teachers, politicians, doctors, police officers, lawyers, teachers, writers, and entrepreneurs. They own homes and have children who are just like my children—children who go to school and are working hard toward a future. Not everyone gets stuck in the projects, but it is a long and tough road out.

The street that I lived on was one of the bright spots of the South Side. It was across the street from the park. The only down side was that Dr. Martin Luther King, Jr. Drive was between the park and us. It was a busy street and we did not have any crossing guards. The nearest traffic light was two blocks away, so we just timed it and ran across the street. For most people, what they did as children they would never allow their own children to do. I dodged cars since I was in the first grade. You would be crazy to think that as a parent I would allow either of my sons to risk their lives dodging cars (some going 50 or 60 miles an hour), just to go to the park! As if all of that was not enough, we ran across rooftops.

There were no houses in my neighborhood, only blocks and blocks of apartment buildings. They were all three stories high and each building was close enough to jump from rooftop to rooftop. We would go up to the third floor in one building and lift the doorway to the rooftop. We would lift each other up through the opening and run across each building, jumping from rooftop to rooftop. An alley separated some buildings, however, it did not matter. We would jump over the alley (three stories up) to the rooftop of the next building.

Once we tired of running from rooftop to rooftop, we would go to the train yards and play on the train tracks, in the open boxcars, and hop onto moving freight trains. The police would chase us away, but we would out run them and come back.

Today, as I look back at growing up in Chicago, I just thank God that I made it out alive. As if it was not dangerous enough running along rooftops or playing on the train tracks or running across busy streets, there were the gangs.

In all of the other dangerous things we did, we had many choices, but with gangs, there were only two choices. You chose to join or you chose not to. Each choice, in places like Chicago, can be a life or death decision; entirely too much weight to put onto a child. When you chose not to join, they would pick on you, beat you up or kill you. When you chose to join one gang, other gangs picked on you, beat you up or killed you. Your own gang pressured you to do things that were morally wrong, that could get you in trouble, sent to jail or killed. All over America, the jails, detention centers, and juvenile lock-up facilities are filled with kids who have made bad choices. And, for many of them, their choices had to do with gangs.

Either way, gangs are bad news for everyone. They destroy people's hopes, dreams, communities, and worse, their lives. They are like a cancer. They eat away at entire communities until there is nothing left; until the buildings are run down and abandoned; until graffiti covers the walls, street signs, store fronts, and cars; until people are afraid to come out of their homes and children are afraid to go to school; until the entire community is plagued by drugs, pain, frustration, and violence.

I will never forget the night that my best friend, Freddie, and I were walking down Calumet Avenue, only a few blocks from where we lived. As we were walking down the street, two boys leaned out of a first-floor window. One of them pointed a shotgun in our faces and shouted, "Represent!" This was a gang's rite of passage. He was asking us to name the gang who controlled Calumet Avenue. The right answer would allow us to pass.

The wrong answer could have caused us to die. Freddie pounded his chest, "Disciple thang." The kid shouted, "Walk on." Two words, *Disciple thang,* allowed us to live. The wrong words could have ended the lives of two kids, walking down the street, minding their own business. In an instant, all of our hopes and dreams could have been destroyed just because we did not know the right answer.

Even though my father worked for the Postal Service and had a good job, he did not have a high school diploma, and he did not make a lot of money. We, like everyone else I grew up with, were poor. My father made enough money so that we wee not on welfare and we did not live in the projects, however, where we lived and how much money we had (or in our case, did not have) was not important. What was important was that my mother and father loved me. My mother had fulfilled her dream of having a child and it was my parents' love that would nurture me to one day discover my dream of becoming a writer.

Most of the people who lived in my neighborhood had no dreams. They did not dream of owning homes, they did not dream of leaving

Chicago—let alone about traveling to other countries or having careers. For so many people, if they had ever had *any* dreams, they were long since gone. People were poor in their spirit. Many of the people in my community had accepted poverty as a condition, which they were powerless to change. They had no dreams and they felt powerless to change their situations. Each day, people fought and died over a few feet of dirt. Drive-by shootings occurred nightly as gangs fought over the right to call a street corner their own. Many of my friends had older brothers who were dead, in jail or on drugs. Rather than following their dreams, most people were stuck in a nightmare.

I was blessed to have a mother who encouraged me to dream and who always told me that I could achieve anything that I could dream of achieving. And, I had a father who gave me the best example. My father did not dream of becoming a millionaire, a teacher, a politician or an entrepreneur. He had simple dreams, all of which he worked his entire life to achieve. He dreamed of leaving the South and finding a job in the North. He dreamed of taking care of his family and about having fun with his friends. He dreamed of returning to where he had grown up and buying his own home. And, he dreamed of his son attending and graduating from college. When I graduated from college my father had realized each of his dreams. Of all of my father's dreams, his dream of seeing me graduate from college was the only one outside of his control. It was also the dream that was the most unlikely to be achieved and the one that had provided him with the greatest joy. However, my graduating from college was the impossible dream, according to my second-grade teacher.

> *I have always believed that the best job that a person could have was to do what he or she loved to do and to get paid for doing it.*
>
> *What is your passion?*

CHAPTER 5

Elementary School

I began kindergarten at Edmund Burke Elementary School. The school was five blocks from where I lived. My grandfather walked me to and from school each day. My grandfather was a big man. He was about six feet nine inches tall and weighed nearly 300 pounds. He had been in jail and most people were afraid of him. When he walked me to school, everybody made a path along the sidewalk. I guess it was kind of like Moses parting the Red Sea.

I only remember two of my teachers from Burke Elementary: Ms. Burke, whom I thought the school was named after, (no one told me that "Edmund" wasn't a lady's name) and Mr. Roberts, my fifth- and sixth-grade teacher, who used to spank us with a paddle for missing spelling words!

I do not remember the principal or any of my other teachers, but I do remember that it was in the second grade that I developed an interest in writing and a passion for talking. I do not believe that my second-grade teacher was particularly fond of my passion for talking. She gave me an *F* in conduct, an *F* in writing, an *F* in reading, and she wrote on my report card "Mychal talks too much!" She also wrote that my reading and language skills were awful and told my mother that she did not think that I would make it out of elementary school!

While I do not remember what my second-grade teacher looked like or much else about second grade, I do remember that I loved making up poems. I was always reciting my poetry to other students and my second-grade teacher was always telling me to "Shut up."

Even though I could not spell and wrote so poorly that I was the only one who could read my writing, I loved to write poetry and I wrote it everywhere—on the walls, on my desk, on paper bags, on toilet paper, and on my hands—everywhere. Not only did I write poetry everywhere, I could write a poem about anything—a fly, a pencil, someone's big head—anything. One of the poems that I wrote in middle school is one of the poems that my company sells today:

A Curious Child

A tug on my arm,
    What could it be?
A child wants to know,
    "How deep is the sea?"
Don't try to ignore it,
    it's already begun.
The next question is,
    "How hot is the sun?"
It won't do any good,
    to pause for a sigh.
Before you can answer,
    "How high is the sky?
Why are mountains so high
    and valleys so low?
Why are cheetahs so fast
    and turtles so slow?
Why do bees make honey?
    How do worms make silk?
Why do chickens lay eggs?
    How do cows give milk?"*
Before you can answer,
    a child question's again.

"Why do we use dollars,
the Japanese use yen?"
We must never forget
that in years gone by,
how we used to question
and others would sigh.
Yet, if they answered each question
with a chuckle and grin,
it would prompt our curiosity
to question again.
We must nurture the brilliance
of the inquisitive child.
No matter how many questions,
let's just answer and smile

— Mychal Wynn

I wrote this poem in middle school and now, my older son, who dreams of becoming an artist, is drawing illustrations for this poem that will be published in a book. I wonder what my second-grade teacher would think about that?

The thing that I remember most about second grade was that my teacher, despite the fact that she did not encourage me to write poetry and she downright discouraged me from talking, read a poem to the class called, "Don't Quit." Hearing her read that poem was the most significant thing

I remember about second grade. I never forgot the title of the poem, "Don't Quit." While I soon forgot the exact wording of the poem, the title "Don't Quit" stuck in my mind. Years later, in high school, I wrote my own poem and entitled it "Don't Quit." *Don't Quit* also became the title of my first book—all because I developed a passion for writing in the second grade and my teacher, unknowingly, inspired me to pursue my writing with even greater passion. What is your passion?

Burke Elementary was an old brick building. The windows had bars on them and most of the windows were broken. The heat did not work in the winter and there was no air conditioning in the spring and summer, so it was always either too cold or too hot. There were a lot of fights, a lot of suspensions, and teachers yelled a lot. Yet, in the midst of it all, there was Mr. Roberts. Mr. Roberts was tall, thin, and had a thick mustache. No one disrespected Mr. Roberts and he never yelled. When Mr. Roberts spoke, everybody listened and when he gave us the "look" we knew that it was time to stop fooling around. We all looked forward to Mr. Roberts' being on recess duty. When he was around, there were no fights or name-calling. Whenever someone rolled their eyes at Mr. Roberts he would say, "You ain't knee high to a duckling. Roll your eyes again and that will be the last time that you roll them!" He would also say, "If you think that an education is expensive, try ignorance!" In class he would always say, "An education is costly, but STUPID is free!" Mr. Roberts believed that we could learn anything. He also told us that he did not care what we looked like, where we came from or how little we knew, he was going to teach us and we were going to learn.

Each Friday morning when he handed back our spelling tests, he made everyone line up along the wall; first the girls, then the boys. Everyone had to hold up their spelling papers with their grades. He went one-by-one and gave the girls one whack on the hand and the boys one whack on the butt for each misspelled word. There were all kinds of hopping around and crying, but the students who had misspelled words became fewer and fewer each week. By the end of the school year, everyone in our classroom could read, write, and spell. We all knew our times tables, as well.

Mr. Roberts also had a dance group where we learned folk dancing. We would all hold hands and dance around like cowboys and cowgirls. The boys wore plaid shirts and string ties. The girls wore plaid dresses. We went all over Chicago dancing in Senior Citizens Homes and at other schools. We even had a "Folk Dance Festival" at school each year. The entire community came to watch us dance to songs like "Sweet Georgia Brown." For many parents, that was the only time they ever came to the school. It was as if a Gospel, Rock or Rap concert was going on. We had people everywhere. I remember my father pushing my grandmother 5 blocks in her wheelchair so that she could see me dance.

You may think that it is silly for poor black children to learn how to folk dance. After all, I do not think that any of us ever did folk dancing again after we graduated from elementary school. However, I believe that Mr. Roberts had a dream that if we could experience success at learning our spelling words and learning folk dancing that we would begin to believe that we could become successful at anything. While most people were dream breakers, and thought that the dreams of poor kids were unrealistic, Mr. Roberts was a dream builder. He told us that with an education, anything was possible. I know that students should not get spanked for missing spelling words, but I also know that Mr. Roberts did not hit us hard enough to hurt us. In his own way, he was just trying to get our attention.

"If you think that an education is expensive, try ignorance.

An education is costly, but STUPID is free!"

CHAPTER 6

Middle School

B y the time I graduated from Edmund Burke Elementary school, Mr. Roberts had me doing math, science, and social studies, and I was excited about school. We would have classroom competitions between the girls and the boys. I was always the smartest boy and I always beat the girls. However, my mother had heard that there were gangs and a lot of fights at Vincennes Middle School, so she decided to send me to a Catholic school. While all of my friends went off to Vincennes, my mother sent me to Corpus Christi Middle School.

At Corpus Christi, I lost all of the enthusiasm about learning that I had gotten from Mr. Roberts. While Mr. Roberts cared about me, I did not feel that the teachers at Corpus Christi did. In fact, I began to get that, "You are a poor kid and you are stupid" feeling again. I realize now that it was not the teachers or the nuns. It was how the students behaved. There was a lot of name-calling, there were a lot of fights, and nobody seemed to be doing anything about it. No one taught us how to work together. No one taught us to believe in ourselves and to talk about our dreams. No one taught us how Corpus Christi Middle School could become a steppingstone toward our dreams and aspirations in life.

I was always getting into trouble. My teeth stuck out and my parents could not afford to pay for braces. Everyone at school called me "Bucky Beaver." I was always getting into fights. It seemed that I was always talking when the teacher was talking or always late for something or always getting into a fight about something stupid. I must have been put out of class or sent to the office at least once a week. Some weeks, I was put out of class every day. I would stand in the corridor and lean against the wall.

One of the nuns would always come by and say to me, "Mr. Mychal, I see that you are holding up the walls again today."

I would respond, "Yes, Sister."

"Mr. Mychal, you must stay in class and learn something if you are to become successful in life."

"Yes, Sister."

"Mr. Mychal, you must make better choices so that you can get an education."

"Yes, Sister."

"Mr. Mychal, you are a bright young man with extraordinary potential."

"Yes, Sister."

"Mr. Mychal, you must try harder to do the right thing."

"Yes, Sister."

"Mr. Mychal, I will see you again tomorrow."

"Yes, Sister."

My mother had to pay tuition for me to attend Catholic School. They should have given her a refund because I spent more time standing in the corridor outside of classes than I did in classes learning.

Despite all of the times that I was put out of class and despite all of the times that my mother was called up to the school, I graduated. The things that I remember most about my two years at Corpus Christi was the nun who always passed me in the corridor when I had been put out of class and Rochelle Parnell.

Rochelle Parnell was my reason for getting up each day and going to school. That is why I know why many students come to school each day, and for them, it is not for learning. Many of them are coming to school because there is a boy or a girl whom they like. In fact, for many boys, that is the only reason that they even wash up in the mornings! I washed up every morning. I put on a little of my father's cologne. I combed my hair and I made sure that my uniform was ironed and starched. I was in love with Rochelle Parnell from the moment that I laid eyes on her. I wrote poems. I sent notes. I did everything that I could to get her attention. Throughout seventh grade Rochelle all but ignored me. I do not know if she was not interested in boys or if she just was not interested in me. She would read my notes and smile. She would read my poems and smile. I was in love and she would just smile. Someone should have helped me to focus on my dreams because all I could do was focus on Rochelle. When she walked into class, my heart would pound. When she sat down, my heart would pound, but she would not give me the time of day.

In the eighth grade, I was not getting into as much trouble. I was still sending my little notes and my little poems to Rochelle and then one day she walked over to my desk and said, "You're cute. Thank you for the poem."

I just sat there expressionless with my mouth open. The girls sitting around me began giggling and singing, "Mychal and Rochelle. Mychal and Rochelle. Mychal and Rochelle." Normally, I would have told them to shut up, but I just sat there thinking, "Rochelle said that I'm cute."

I know that guys in school today are so cool that they would never behave as I did. I did not care what other people would have done or what other people may have thought. I was in love with Rochelle Parnell. I had been writing poems for, and sending notes to her for over a year and now she was paying attention.

Rochelle was my girlfriend from the eighth grade and through most of high school. During that period of time in my life she was also my best friend. Rochelle and I, like so many other people whom I grew up with in Chicago, eventually lost touch and drifted apart. Although Rochelle was my best friend, we never talked about our dreams. I do not know what her dreams were or what dreams she ultimately pursued in life. I do not remember a single assignment, discussion, or project at Corpus Christi that involved talking about our dreams. Rochelle was one of my most significant memories about Corpus Christi and I do not even know what her dreams were.

Who are your friends and what are their dreams?

CHAPTER 7

High School

My mother, despite all of the problems that I had at Corpus Christi, was determined to send me on to an all-boys Catholic High School. De La Salle was one of the best high schools in the city of Chicago. It was where Mayor Richard Daley, a former Mayor of Chicago, went to school.

De La Salle High School could have been the ultimate launching pad toward my dreams and aspirations. De La Salle had a national reputation for academic excellence. If I had taken my schoolwork seriously and paid less attention to what my friends were saying about me, I could have received a college scholarship to anywhere in the country. However, I found myself in the ninth grade and still no one had ever asked what my dreams and aspirations were!

The neighborhood boys made fun of my uniform and called me "Mayor" because the mayor of Chicago had gone to De La Salle. Since De La Salle was an all-boys school, they called me a lot of other names as well. The girls said that I went to a "sissy school."

I found myself paying more attention to what people were saying than about how attending one of the best high schools in Chicago could help me to become successful in life. Even though my dreams were not clear and even though no one had ever asked me what my dreams were, my parents had gotten me into a school that none of my friends could afford to attend. No one had ever sat down and talked to me about what I liked to do, what I might be interested in learning, what I might be interested in achieving or where I might be interested in going in life.

I believe that if someone had sat down with me and talked to me about my interests, if my parents and teachers would have just taken the time to get to know me, they would have discovered what my passions were (writing and talking) and they could have helped me to understand how my passions could have become my dreams. If I could have understood how school could help me to pursue my dreams, I would not have allowed my friends to distract me. Instead, most of my teachers saw my passion for writing as a distraction, my passion for talking as troublesome, and did nothing to help me to discover how my passions (writing and talking) could become my career (writing and talking!).

I was not a bad student, I just was not a good student. I never put in as much effort as I could have. I had brilliant days, days when I scored 100 percent on every test—on other days, I failed every test. I turned in brilliant book reports and research papers when I was interested, but I did not turn in any papers when I was not interested.

I tell my older son, Mychal-David, that the worst place to get advice is from his friends. They do not know any more than he does! In fact, most of them know less. However, if he is going to listen to me, to benefit from my experiences, I also have to listen to him. He and I talk a lot about his dreams and aspirations. When he was in middle school he dreamed of becoming an artist, illustrator or computer animator. He was certain that he wanted to attend the Savannah College of Art and Design. However, by the time that he had reached the eleventh grade he had decided that he wanted to attend a traditional four-year college where he could study more than just art. He eventually decided to apply to Amherst College, the top liberal arts college in the United States. Now he is talking about going to school for a year in Japan and eventually going to law school. As he learns more, he will desire to do more. As he experiences more, he will discover new dreams, new aspirations, and new opportunities. He may even decide to go into politics and run for President one day.

All of my experiences help me to understand my sons. In many ways, they are very much like me. However, I am not at all like my teachers at De La Salle High School. I push my sons to study and to do their work, but I also help them to understand that what they are doing in school today can help them to achieve their dreams tomorrow. I am also tougher on my sons than my parents were on me. Report cards are serious business in our home. Our goal is always straight *A*'s. Neither of my sons is a straight *A* student, but neither is ever far from it. While you may not always achieve your goals, you should always have goals that you are trying to achieve. My philosophy is simple, "An *A* student should get *A*'s, *B* students should get better, *C* students should work harder, and *D* students should spend more time hanging around *A* and *B* students!" I also tell both of my sons that school is their J-O-B. Do the work and get paid with the grades. I have never forgotten what Mr. Roberts told us, "If you think that an education is expensive, try IGNORANCE."

When my older son was in the seventh grade, he received 5 *A*'s and 2 *B*'s. My younger son, who is now in the seventh grade, has just received his first semester grades—5 *A*'s and 2 *B*'s. Their grades are much better than mine were—not because they are smarter than I was, but because my wife and I are pushing them and we have high expectations. We are helping each of them to develop a balance between schoolwork and socializing. Our older son was in the gifted and talented program and all his classes were advanced classes. So too, is his younger brother. Our older son was chosen to represent his middle school in the countywide *Mathmania Competition* and in the *Economics Quiz Bowl* (which they won). In addition to his academic recognition he won numerous art awards for his drawings and illustrations. He was a popular kid and like many of his friends, he would have been content to get *C's* instead of *A's* and *B's*. However, living in our home, everybody has a job. His, was school. Now, his younger brother is in the Jr. Beta Club, plays football, is in the Chorus, and is expected to excel academically.

When our younger son was in the first grade, he dreamed of becoming a motorcycle racer, professional soccer player, professional baseball player, and a speaker, like me. I do not know if he can ride a motorcycle, but he is a good athlete and he loves to talk. He reads and does homework every night, just like his older brother did. In fact, he probably does more homework than some of the students whom I speak to in high schools and he reads a lot more than most of the students I speak to in elementary, middle, or high school. He, too, is in training. He is preparing to pursue his dreams, whatever they may become. Learning how to read, how to write, and how to solve problems is not an option. Learning how to hit a ball, dunk a ball or kick a ball *are* options. Schoolwork comes before socializing. Homework comes before after-school activities. If he does not follow his teachers' instructions and do his work in school, then he does not go to football practice after school. If you do not do your job, then you do not earn your pay (in his situation the right to play football). If you want to become a better hitter, you have to practice. If you want to become a faster runner, you have to practice. If you want to become a better musician, you have to practice. If you want to get smarter, you have to exercise your brain! I wish that when I was in high school, the principal and teachers had known how to help me to discover my dreams so I would understand how focusing more attention on my schoolwork and less on the advice of my friends would have helped me to achieve my dreams.

What I have learned is, "If you do not have a dream, then you cannot have a plan!" While no plan is perfect, not having a plan is like sailing across the Atlantic Ocean with no compass, no navigational equipment, and two months of supplies for a three-month trip. While you may survive and actually make it to land somewhere, you most likely will not survive and most probably will be lost at sea.

If someone in the second grade had seen my passion for writing and talking as indicators that I may have a dream of becoming a writer or a professional speaker, then they could have helped me and my parents to begin developing my plan. I may have gone to Corpus Christi Middle School with passion and a purpose. I may have entered De La Salle High School focusing on writing, speech and debate, journalism, or communications and paid less attention to what my friends were saying. And, I may have had a plan for going to college to study journalism, for my passion for writing, and business, for my desire to become a professional speaker. If you have a dream, then you must have a plan. Without a plan, it is easy to make bad choices. Like so many of the students whom I talk to in schools today, I did not go to school each day with passion and I did not pursue my schoolwork with purpose.

Both of my sons have attended schools, camps, and summer programs to nurture their gifts as part of a long-term plan to pursue their dreams. My wife and I inspired our older son to picture his first-grade stick people as a long-term dream of becoming an artist. He did not come home from school in the first grade and proclaim, "Mom, Dad, I have a dream of becoming an artist!" Few young people start out in elementary school with any clear focus on what their future dreams and aspirations are. However, almost every student in every school has a passion for something, albeit writing, talking, drawing, sports, science, math, English, taking pictures, acting or playing video games. Everyone has a passion for something. While my older son played baseball and video games, studied martial arts, and engaged in countless other things that young people do, he had a *passion* for drawing.

It all began the summer we moved to Atlanta from California. Two of my son's older cousins, Marcus and Oscar, spent the summer with us. At the time, Mychal-David was three years old and his cousin Marcus was seven years old. Marcus loved to draw comic book characters and Mychal-David would try to imitate what Marcus did. His three-year-old drawings were awful, but that did not matter. He was not drawing to impress anyone. He was not drawing to turn his work in to his preschool teacher for a gold star. In the beginning, he just wanted to try to draw as well as his older cousin. However, three years later, at age six, he was still drawing. Recognizing that drawing was becoming a passion for him, my wife and I began helping him to develop his plan, which included art classes after school, summer art camp, and "How to Draw Cartoons" videos. Our family eventually moved from Marietta, Georgia, to St. Petersburg, Florida, so he could attend a public magnet school for the arts. He attended elementary and middle school in Florida where he perfected his artistic talents every day. He had two full periods of art, five days a week, taught by professional artists. He illustrated the characters from some of the books his class studied in language arts. He built models in science, drew maps in social studies, and understood that math was helping him learn how to solve problems like the types of problems he would face while running his own graphic arts company, art gallery, animation studio or publishing company. He attended conferences and book signings with me where he spoke to professional artists and art gallery owners. He envisioned himself signing his artwork, greeting cards, and books. Nearing the end of middle school we moved back to Georgia where he attended North Springs High School, which offered a magnet program in art, math, and science.

My younger son, Jalani, while in the first grade, was learning how to become a storyteller, since he loves to talk, and practiced drama and acting. As a family, we were on "Dream Alert" as we waited for Jalani to reveal his passions so we could help him to affirm his dreams and to begin developing his plan. A great athlete and a wonderful person, we witnessed a new gift during the fifth grade as he performed as Nick Bottom, in Shakespeare's, *A Midsummer Night's Dream*. With his awesome performance and beautiful voice, Jalani will have many options and many dreams—acting, athletics, entrepreneurship, singing, or writing. My passion for writing began in the second grade. My older son's passion for drawing began in the first grade. Now, as a middle school student, Jalani's gifts may just be greater than us all.

Each of my sons may change his dreams later in life, but no one can take away the knowledge they are gaining today. I get angry when I think about all of the time I could have been writing poems, short stories, screen plays or novels while I was in school. Everything I needed was right there: encyclopedias, dictionaries, reference books, and teachers who could help me edit and correct my grammar. It was all right there in the school, but I did not know how to say, "I WANT TO LEARN HOW TO BECOME A WRITER!"

Even though I eventually discovered my dreams, and even though I am now living my dreams, middle school and high school would have been so different if someone had just sat down and talked to me.

I continued to plod right along at De La Salle High School until my sophomore year. At the beginning of my sophomore year there was a kid, named Reggie, who was bigger and stronger than me, who did not like poor kids (like me), and who always found a way to step up in my face. His locker was next to mine and he found a reason to bully me every day. Here I was, a poor kid from the South Side, whose parents were trying to send him to a good school so that he could have a successful future, and here was a rich kid and his crew of rich kids who were intent on making my life miserable. Not only did I have to deal with my friends talking about me in the neighborhood on my way to school, but I also had to deal with people talking about me once I got to school. I had escaped the street gangs only to run into this new gang of spoiled rich kids.

Every day, they talked about and bullied me, in the cafeteria, in the gymnasium, in the locker room, and at my locker between classes. It seemed that everywhere I turned they were there. I told my mother and father about it. They told me to try to avoid them and not let it bother me. I told my teacher about it and he told me that he would speak to them. Whatever he said did not work because nothing changed. I went to the principal and told him. He also said that he would speak to them, which he did. Whatever he said just made them angry because the next day, Reggie told me he was going to kick my butt and send my poor behind back to the projects (and I did not even live in the projects)!

That day after school, I saw Reggie with his posse so I ran across the school's parking lot and down the street to the 35th Street Train Station. I was in a hurry so I did not have time to pay. I jumped over the turnstile and ran toward the escalator to the platform. Before I reached the escalator, I felt someone grab my jacket from behind. The next thing I knew, Reggie was twisting my left arm behind my back. He choked me until I lost consciousness. When I awoke, I was lying on the ground and Reggie was sitting on my chest slapping me in the face. As he slapped me he kept telling me how I had gotten him in trouble with the principal.

I had enough of this nonsense, "Boy, you had better get off me!" I said. But no matter how hard I tried, I could not get up. Finally, the train came and people started coming down the escalator. Reggie got up and told me, "Boy, you'd better not ever come back to this school."

I may not have thought much of going to De La Salle, however, I was not going to allow him to keep me from going to school, and I was tired of being intimidated.

My shoulder was so badly swollen that I could not go back to school for nearly a week. I could not tell my mother what had happened and I was not going to go back to school and tell the principal. I left home each day that week pretending to go to school. I went over to Lake Michigan where I sat in the park and wrote poetry. I was waiting for my shoulder to heal so I could go back to school for a showdown with Reggie.

Monday morning, I got up to go to school with a plan. I was going to walk up to Reggie in the hallway before class and I was going to punch him in the eye in front of everybody. I knew that I had to punch him squarely in the eye so it would turn black. I was going to punch him in the hallway before class because I needed someone to break it up after I hit him.

As I was walking through the corridor, I saw Reggie coming. I squeezed my fist. As I approached him, he began to smile as if remembering the train station incident. I kept walking, thinking about what Muhammad Ali used to say, "Float like a butterfly and sting like a bee." I took the smirk right off of his face. I punched him in the right eye—squarely in the eye.

Now, I am not suggesting that anyone should go to school and punch someone in the eye. I certainly will not tolerate my children fighting at school for any reason. Fighting in school is a criminal offense and can get you suspended from school or thrown in jail. In most schools, there are counselors, crisis intervention specialists, teachers, administrators, and law enforcement personnel who can help young people avoid situations like what I was going through. For me, however, at that point in my life, no one was listening. No one was helping me and I did not see any way out. I was not going to spend the next two years being bullied everyday at school. So I punched Reggie in the eye.

After I hit him I did not say anything and I did not go anywhere. I just watched him fall down onto the floor holding his eye. I was standing over him when one of the coaches grabbed me and pulled me away. They sent us both to the principal's office. My mother had to come to school to get me. When she got there, they all found out I had been cutting school for the past five days. The principal told my mother he did not like to give up on young people, but if I had another fight, he would permanently expel me from school.

After that, Reggie's eye was swollen for nearly a month. Everybody in school was talking about it and nobody bothered me anymore. In fact, the talk throughout the school was that anybody crazy enough to hit Reggie in the eye was just plain crazy!

While people left me alone, things did not get much better at school. A month later, I got into another fight in PE and the principal called my mother again. I was expelled from school. Still, no one had ever asked me about my dreams.

> *You have to have a dream before you can develop a plan.*

Chapter 8

A New High School

Du Sable High School was the public high school in my neighborhood. If De La Salle was the best high school in the city, Du Sable was the worst. Du Sable was across the street from the projects and the scene of constant cafeteria fights, gang fights, girl fights, and just fights in general. The previous fall, there was a shootout in the hallway between rival gangs. I had been expelled from De La Salle just before Christmas, so I did not have to start attending Du Sable until January.

For most students, the only way to survive at Du Sable was to join a gang, join the band, join one of the athletic teams or be a cheerleader. Since I did not want to join a gang, I could not play a musical instrument, and I definitely was not going to be a cheerleader, I decided that I would play football. By January, the school had quieted down a great deal. The real troublemakers had been suspended for the rest of the school year or had been sent to jail. Everyone from my neighborhood went to Du Sable, so I knew a lot of people. My first day of classes, I saw a lot of faces I had not seen since elementary school. All in all, Du Sable was not too bad. At least here, no one made fun of me for being poor. We were all poor!

Despite knowing people from the neighborhood and from elementary school, I knew that to ensure my survival at Du Sable I had two choices. Join a gang or join the football team. I chose to try out for the football team.

At the first practice, Coach Bonner opened with his simple philosophy. "I have 50 uniforms. My job is to run you into the ground until I only have 50 people left standing. Those 50 will be my football team." Here I was, standing in the gymnasium at just over 150 pounds, with over 300 of some of the biggest, meanest, toughest thugs in Chicago. For some of these guys, making the football team was a part of their dream of getting out of poverty and out of the projects. A football scholarship was their ticket to college. Others, simply wanted the opportunity to take all of their anger, frustration, and aggression out on somebody. They did not want to just tackle you, they wanted to break you. At 150 pounds, my dream was just surviving Du Sable!

De La Salle and Reggie were not looking too bad right about now. If they would have taken me back, I would have gone back. In fact, if my mother had brought me over to Du Sable before she put me into De La Salle, there was no way I would have allowed myself to get kicked out. Had I lost my mind or was I simply stuck in a nightmare? "Please, somebody wake me." I was awakened by a whistle, "Alright, you sissy's. Get your butts in gear and follow the team captain. You're going to get a tour of the school."

We ran out of the door of the gymnasium, down the hall, up the stairs to the third floor, down the hall, down the stairs to the second floor, down the hall, down the stairs to the first floor, down the hall, and up the stairs again. We continued doing this until our tongues were wagging and guys were falling out. By the time we were done, we were down to about 250 guys. We finally returned to the gym and Coach Bonner yelled, "All right. Let's see who else wants to go home? Hit the floor and give me sit-ups until I tell you to stop." We did so many sit-ups that my abs were burning. Every time someone slowed down, Coach Bonner yelled, "I'm not tired. Give me some more." What did he mean, "I'm not tired?" He should not have been tired. He was not doing anything but screaming at us! One by one as these tough guys gave up or just gave out, Coach Bonner told them, "Get your stuff and get out of here." Only about 150 came back the next day and we started all over again.

We went on like this, day after day. We ran, we did push-ups, we did sit-ups, we did jumping jacks, we did sprints in the gym, and I had not seen a football yet. By the end of two weeks of this, there were only about 100 guys left standing. As more and more guys gave up each day, Coach Bonner would yell, "Pack your stuff up and get your butts out of here."

By the end of the tenth grade I was one of the fifty left standing. I was going to play football for the Du Sable High School "Panthers." I still had not gained much weight and I had earned the nickname, "Malnutrition."

When I tried out for the football team, my dream was to make the team. I did. My goal was to be able to go to school without anybody bothering me, and no one bothered me. By the end of summer practice, I was the number two tailback. I had put on a little weight since spring training, so they no longer called me "Malnutrition." However, I was so slow they gave me another nickname, "Slow Motion."

I had earned a position on the Du Sable High School varsity football team. No one bothered me and I had made a lot of friends. I achieved my goal. Two games into the season, during eleventh grade, I quit the football team. My dream was to become a writer, not a football player. I joined the football team only to ensure my survival at Du Sable High School. Even though I had made some friends, I did not have a lot in common with the other players. I did not share their dreams. I did not share their aspirations. I did not share their values. Many of the guys would brag about getting a girl pregnant. They would brag about beating up or bullying people. They thought it was cool not to do their schoolwork.

Even when I did not do my schoolwork, I did not think that it was cool. I was uninterested sometimes and lazy most times. They did not want to do anything in life but play football, hang out, party, and get drunk on the weekends. None of the players lived in my neighborhood. Most of them lived in the projects. Most of the projects in Chicago were the types of places where if you did not live there, you did not go there. In fact, if you lived in one building, you could not go into another building without a fight or worst, a shooting.

One day after practice, I took off my equipment, turned in my uniform, and never went back to football practice again. When the players asked why I had quit the team, I just told them my mother said I could not play anymore. Coach Bonner never called me into his office to talk about why I had quit the team. In fact, he never talked to me again. As far as I was concerned, Coach Bonner was just another person who did not talk to me and who did not listen to me. I did not have anyone to talk to. My dad did not even know I had been on the football team. My mother knew I had been going to football practice after school since spring, but when I stopped going to practice she just assumed the season was over.

That experience, more than anything else, taught me not to quit anything. That is why I will not allow my sons to quit once they begin something. No matter what it is, they have to stick it out to the end. Mychal-David took Ho Shin Do Karate when he was four years old. About halfway through his training, he decided he was tired and did not want to continue. However, I would not let him quit. When he first enrolled in Ho Shin Do, his goal was to earn his black belt. My wife and I took him to class three nights a week for four years and we would not allow him to quit until he earned his back belt. One by one—white, yellow, green, blue, purple, red, brown, and black. He earned his belts one-by-one over four years. When he was eight years old, he received his black belt. Shortly after receiving his black belt, he decided to stop training for a while. We allowed him stop training because he had reached his goal. The same thing happened when he wanted to learn how to ride a bicycle.

I took him to the school's parking lot with his new bicycle. He rode and fell, I pushed, he rode, and fell. This went on all day. Fortunately, he was wearing wrist pads, elbow pads, kneepads, and a helmet. His pads were scratched up. The bicycle was scratched up. He was falling down and crying. He wanted to give up, but I would not let him. He had set a goal to learn how to ride a bicycle. Finally, just before the sun went down, I gave him a push and he was on his way. Throughout elementary and middle school he went to the aggressive skating rink where he did flips on roller blades and flew off ramps. He fell down a lot, but he never quit until he perfected his moves. That is how life is. No matter how many times you fall down, you have to continue to get up. Quitting should not be an option.

Everyone has to learn how to set goals and to work toward them. Everyone has to learn not to quit. I realized that I quit the Du Sable High School football team because I had set my goal too low. Remember, my goal was to make the football team. It was not to start. It was not to win a championship. It was not to become a professional football player. It was not to get a college scholarship. It was to *make* the football team. After I had achieved my goal of making the team, I found myself confronted with new decisions and I did not have anyone to give me advice.

My advice to you is to set your goals high! Find someone who will listen to you and tell them about your goals, your dreams, your passions, and your aspirations. Stay focused on your goals and don't quit!

Begin with the end in mind.

Identify a long-term goal and begin working backwards to set college, high school, middle school, and elementary school goals.

Then, set yearly, monthly, and weekly goals for each school year.

CHAPTER 9

Graduation

I had pretty much survived my last year at Du Sable. I was no longer getting into trouble like I was in middle school or when I was attending De La Salle High School. The strange thing about high school is that a lot of people begin to take it seriously in the twelfth grade. They realize that this is it. Just a few more months and they will be forced to decide what they want to do with their lives. This is probably one of the most confusing times in the lives of young people; however, many of them, like me, have been fooling around, not doing much, and not learning much. Now they are confronted with serious long-term life decisions.

The final year of high school should be one of the happiest times in a young person's life. It marks the year for taking giant steps toward lifetime dreams. You should be focused on going to college, trade school, into the armed forces or somewhere else in life. It is important to know where you are going so you can enjoy the final year of high school by taking pictures and putting together your scrapbook, saying good-bye to teachers, and looking forward to the prom. The main focus should be directed toward the future.

If that is the dream about the way it is supposed to be, then I was beginning my final year of high school in a nightmare. I still did not know what I wanted to do with my life. I just knew I wanted to get out of high school. I did not begin my final year of high school with a goal of going to college or of becoming a famous writer or of building a multi-million dollar publishing company or of transforming schools or of helping people discover their dreams. I wanted to get out of Chicago. I wanted to get out of poverty. The choice that appeared to make the most sense was to go to college. I would be out of Du Sable High School and I could leave Chicago. Some of the college dormitories were a lot bigger than my current bedroom and they were located in communities a lot nicer than where I lived.

As my final year of high school dragged on, I was more and more concerned that I was getting closer and closer to graduation and I still did not have a plan. I knew I was going to college, if for no other reason than no one in my family had ever gone to, let alone, graduated from college. While most of my friends were going into the Armed Forces, I had a huge Afro and no intent of cutting it off.

What was I going to study in college? That question, prompted me to go and see my high school guidance counselor, Mr. Jones, for help. I knocked on his door. Mr. Jones sat in an old chair, behind an old desk, in an old school. The old wooden door to his office had papers tacked all over the bottom of the door. The top of the door was glass, and printed across the top of the glass in big gold letters were the words, "Guidance Counselor."

I knocked on the door. I could see Mr. Jones sitting behind his desk with papers everywhere. He looked up and motioned me into the office. Mr. Jones asked, "What can I do for you?" "Mr. Jones I want to be a writer," I told him. "Can you tell me how to become a writer?" Mr. Jones did not ask me about the type of writer I wanted to become. He did not ask why I wanted to become a writer. He did not suggest that we look at colleges with good journalism programs. Mr. Jones asked, "What kind of grades are you getting?" I told him that I had *A's* in everything but English and Biology. I had a *C* in English and an *F* in Biology.

When the school year began, I loved Biology. I had a great teacher and she could tell that I loved Biology. I was getting *A's* on everything, and then I made a dumb choice. I went to the back of the room. There are a lot of kids who want to sit in the back of the classroom. I call them the "Back of the Room Kids." In each of my classes where teachers allowed you to pick your own seat, I always sat in the front of the room. After all, I was a senior. This was my last year of high school and it was time to get serious about my education (I now knew that I should have been serious about my education when I was in elementary school).

In middle school and my first two years of high school, I did not take schoolwork seriously. By the third and fourth years of high school, I woke up and began to pay attention. I began to realize that I would have to get a real job. That is why I tell both of my sons that school is their J-O-B. If they do well at this job, it will help them to get a better job when they get out of school. A part-time job pays enough money to buy sneakers or tickets to the movies but a better job pays enough to pay the rent, light bill, gas bill, car payment, gas, insurance, groceries, clothes, doctor and dental bills. The ticket to a better job was a college degree.

In the eleventh grade I began to see four groups of people beginning to develop in school. One group was made up of students who were working hard, getting good grades, and planning to go to a four-year college or university. Another group was talking about trade school, Junior College or joining the armed forces (Army, Navy, Marines, Air Force). The third group was not talking about anything and did not have a clue as to what they were going to do after graduation. Maybe they would get married, get a job or just stay at home until they either figured out what to do or their parents forced them to get out. The fourth group was just chill'n and hanging out. They were the gang bangers, street hustlers or thugs. Most of them had been to jail or were going to jail. Many people in this group did not believe they were going to live past 21, so they were not planning on a long future and they were not making good decisions. The only thing each of these four groups had in common was that all of the people within each of these groups got to choose whether or not to join that particular group. Some people had more choices than others, but they all had a choice.

All four groups were represented in my biology class. Most of the people in the first group (the group planning to go to college) were girls. Most of the people in the last two groups were boys. Most of them were either on the football team or in a gang. Some of them were on the football team *and* in a gang. Even though I was no longer playing football, I knew all of these guys, and, because I was friends with them, no one bothered me at school. They all sat in the back of the room clowning around. I did the dumbest thing. I went to the back of the room with them. My teacher did everything she could to help me. However, the more she tried to help and encourage me, the more they teased me and called me a teacher's pet. Eventually, I began clowning around and not doing my work like them. I wish that somebody had told me, "Boy, you had better wake up and recognize. These guys are not going to pay your bills or help you to achieve your dreams. You had better follow your dreams instead of following these clowns!"

My biology teacher eventually gave up on me and my grades went down. I stopped going to class. I failed biology because I was not smart enough to make the right choice. I could remember Mr. Roberts holding his paddle and standing in front of my fifth-grade class, "If you think that an education is expensive, try ignorance." The faces are older now, but you will find many of the faces of the group in the back of the room at the Cook County Jail, Illinois State Penitentiary or on street corners around Chicago. They made bad choices. While I made a bad choice and moved to the back of the room in biology, fortunately, I chose the front of the room in all of my other classes and I chose to join the group of people who were going to college. If I had not begun making the right choices, instead of writing this book, I may have been one of the faces standing on a street corner in Chicago, lying dead in the streets or wasting my life away in the Illinois State Penitentiary. Life is just a series of choices.

When I asked Mr. Jones to tell me how I could follow my dream of becoming a writer, he pushed himself back from his desk, pulled his eye glasses down on his nose, and looked over the frames at me. "There ain't no jobs for no Negro writers, but you have good grades in math. You could be an engineer. Why don't you come back in a couple of days. I will pull your records and we can find a good college with a good engineering program."

I went back to see Mr. Jones a few days later. He had reviewed my grades and ACT scores. He told me that with my grades and ACT scores, I could probably get into the Illinois Institute of Technology's Engineering program. He gave me a brochure and an application to IIT. We did not talk any more about my dream of becoming a writer or the fact that I was determined to leave Chicago. I remember leaving his office and throwing the brochure and application into the trash on my way to class. I did, however, follow Mr. Jones' advice to concentrate on becoming an engineer.

I joined the school's yearbook staff as a photographer. I loved taking pictures and being a part of another team, since I was not playing football anymore. During the spring of my senior year, I went to Chicago's Annual College Fair to take pictures for the school's yearbook. While taking pictures at the fair, I met a man at a booth who represented Northeastern University in Boston, Massachusetts. He explained to me that Northeastern had over 50,000 students and was the largest private university in the United States.

Northeastern had a five-year cooperative education program, which was the largest in the world. The co-op program meant that a student could work in a full-time job within a field of study for six months out of the year. The money earned could help to pay for college tuition and would provide two years of full-time work experience by graduation. Northeastern had one of the best engineering schools in the country and loans and scholarships were available to help needy students. The man gave me an admissions application, an application fee waiver (that means that if you are poor you can submit the application without the $25.00 fee), financial-aid application, brochures, a button, a ruler, and a Northeastern bag!

I was sold. I had to go to school where I could earn enough money to get through school. I had performed so poorly during my three years of high school that I could not qualify for any academic scholarships. This way, I would be able to earn enough money to pay my way through college, and, Northeastern was in Boston, nearly a thousand miles and a lifetime away from Chicago. When I returned to school on the following Monday, the first thing I did was to get the United States map to find out exactly how far Boston was from Chicago (994 miles). I wanted to get as far away from Chicago as I could. By that Friday, I had my admissions and financial-aid applications (together with my fee waiver) in the mail. I did not tell anyone I was applying to Northeastern, not even my mother and father.

A couple of months later, I received a letter from Northeastern. I had been issued a "conditional acceptance." The condition was that I could not enroll in the fall, however, if I took and passed a semester of physics, I could enroll in the winter quarter. This was great because I did not have any money anyway. I had time to work, save money, take physics, pack my bags, and get out of Chicago.

Remember what I said before about needing a dream in order to have a plan? If becoming an engineer had really been my dream, instead of waiting on Mr. Jones' advice, I could have had a plan long before I entered high school. I could have researched college engineering programs while I was in middle school. I could have identified the colleges with the best programs where I stood a good chance of getting accepted. I could have identified sources of financial aid and scholarships. In other words, I could have had a plan long before my senior year of high school and my life would not have been guided by fate.

It also occurred to me that my teachers and counselors at Du Sable could have at least spent more time in class talking to us about what we needed to do to prepare for college. Most of my classmates were like me. No one in our families had gone to college. All of us were poor. None of us had any real plans for our futures. Most of our friends were dropping out of school. The amazing thing was that we were still in school and most of us were determined to do something with our lives. We just did not know what to do and we desperately needed a plan.

The school's idea of a plan was to have us walk around on a college campus. Four bus loads of students from Du Sable took a trip to the University of Illinois in Urbana-Champaign. We did not do any schoolwork to prepare for the trip. We did not develop a list of questions to ask once we arrived on campus. We had not talked about what our dreams were and how the University of Illinois could possibly help us to achieve our dreams. We did not have any schoolwork related to the trip once we returned to school. All that I can recall is that we got onto the buses, rode a couple of hours to the University of Illinois, got off of the buses, clowned around all day, got back onto the buses, and returned to school.

While my plan was far from perfect, the fact was, I had a plan while most of my friends had no plans whatsoever. I got a job working part-time (at night) at the Main Post Office in downtown Chicago. I worked from 10:00 p.m. until 2:30 a.m., sorting mail. Sometimes, when the sorting was slow, I had to unload the mail trucks down on the docks. The docks were on the Chicago River and it was so cold it felt as if I was in Alaska instead of Chicago. I dragged myself to school every morning. I did not care how tired I was, I had a dream that was within my power to achieve. I dreamed of leaving Chicago. With the money earned from my job at the Post Office and the letter of acceptance from Northeastern, I was just one physics class away from realizing my dream.

I did not go to my high school prom or to my high school graduation. A lot of my friends had dropped out of school by then. Going to Du Sable every day was not at all like the cute little television shows about high school life. There were no groups of giggling girls and handsome athletes standing around talking about the colleges they had been accepted to. There were no groups of National Merit Scholars standing around talking about all of the academic scholarships they had earned. We did not have meetings where college recruiters came in to tell us about their wonderful programs. We did not spend time in class talking about the wonderful futures awaiting us upon graduation. A lot of the boys already had criminal records. A lot of the girls were pregnant or already had babies. People were planning on getting married or getting jobs, but not planning on going to college. Of the 500 students who entered ninth grade at Du Sable high school, less than 50 were scheduled to graduate.

At the end of the school year, in June, 1974, I received my diploma and waved good-bye to Du Sable High School. Out of the ninth-grade class of 500 students I was one of fifteen planning to attend a four-year college or university.

I continued working at the Post Office and began taking physics and calculus classes at Kennedy-King Jr. College on the south side of Chicago. I got an *A* in physics and a *B* in calculus. In January, 1975, I packed my trunk, bought a one-way plane ticket, kissed my mama good-bye, hugged my daddy, got on the airplane, and said good-bye to

Chicago. No one asked what my dreams were and after my last conversation with Mr. Jones, I was determined not to tell anyone, either.

> *Good choices result from having good information. Your friends are usually the worst sources of information whose advice usually leads to bad choices!*

CHAPTER 10

I Made It!

There was no big celebration after graduating from high school or when I left Chicago. We did not have a big family get-together to celebrate my going away to college. No one else in my family had gone to college and no one but my mama and daddy thought that it was a big deal. In fact, the rest of my family just started calling me "College Boy." When I got accepted to college, no one at Du Sable made a big deal either. That has always bothered me. We made a big deal out of winning football games. We made a big deal out of winning basketball games. We filled the gymnasium with students, the band played, the cheerleaders cheered, and we made a big deal about opening the football and basketball seasons. Well, here we were, a handful of people out of the 500 who had begun in the ninth grade at Du Sable, who had graduated from high school and been accepted into college, and they did not even post a list with our names on it. Of the fifty or so students who had graduated, only about fifteen actually planned on going to a four-year college or university. Fifteen people out of the 500 who entered the ninth grade were going to college and no one thought it was a big deal. If *they* did not make a big deal out of my going to college, my dad did. He told everybody who would listen, "My boy is going to college. My boy is going to become an engineer." Everywhere we went, "Hi, my boy is going to college." He told everybody at work; he told everybody in the barbershop; he told everybody in the neighborhood. My mother gave out a big sigh of relief. I had not joined a gang. I had not gone to jail. I had not gotten anyone pregnant. I had graduated from high school. And, I had survived Chicago.

My parents took me to O'Hara airport where I checked my trunk. It contained everything that I owned. I was not planning on returning to Chicago to live, only to visit. When I kissed my mama and hugged my daddy good-bye, I had no idea that I was about to take a giant step closer to realizing my dreams.

Sitting in the airport, waiting to board the airplane, I began reflecting on my life in Chicago. I began thinking about all of the people from Du Sable who were now working or living at home, hustling, in jail or standing on street corners. Only a few of us had made it out of poverty. Only a few of us still had dreams. I then reflected on all of the faces in Mrs. Burke's kindergarten classroom at Edmund Burke Elementary School. I still have my kindergarten class picture. Derek Strong, Michael Pierce, Vickie Burke, Pamela Simms, and Jacqueline McKenzie. Where were they now? What happened to their hopes and their dreams? Less than six months out of high school, I was already out of touch with almost everyone I had gone to school with.

I boarded the airplane for the flight to Boston. It was the first time I had ever been on an airplane. When the plane took off, I was sad that I was leaving my mother and father, but I was glad I was leaving Chicago. Do not misunderstand me, Chicago is a great city. In fact, now, I love going to Chicago. One day, I may even choose to live there again. I would like to experience living where Oprah Winfrey lives. I would like to help the kids who now live in the area where I grew up to understand that where Oprah lives is only a dream away.

As the airplane cruised across the country at 30,000 feet, I thought about the only other occasions during which I had ever been out of Chicago. Every summer, for as long as I could remember, we took our annual family trip to Memphis. My father and mother, my aunt, my cousins, and I drove to Memphis and spent the summer at my grandparents' home. My father and his sister (my aunt) were raised by their grandparents, Big Mama and Big Daddy. Big Mama was big! She stood about 6 feet 5 inches tall. She was mixed with Cherokee Indian and had one long braid of hair that hung down her back to her waist. Big Daddy was big, too. But instead of being tall, he was wide. Their house was on the corner. They had a garden, a chicken yard, and a chicken house.

My mother and father had relatives everywhere. In fact, in one area, nearly everyone on the block was related in some way—first cousins, second cousins, third cousins, great aunts and uncles.

There were no apartments and no projects. Everybody owned their own home and some houses had been in the family for generations. They were the only people I had known who owned their own homes. We lived in an apartment in Chicago and all of my cousins lived in the projects. Unlike Chicago, at that time, in Memphis there were no gangs and no drive-by shootings. The only shooting was done by Big Daddy who sat on the porch each evening with his shotgun shooting chicken hawks. All of my cousins from Chicago called all of my cousins from Memphis "country," but we all enjoyed picking fruits and vegetables from the garden, feeding the chickens, and going fishing. No one wanted to leave at the end of the summer. No one was anxious to go back to Chicago. No one was anxious to go back to the projects.

I started thinking about my cousin, Gregory. He and I were more like brothers than cousins. We went everywhere and did everything together. We were the same age and we were always getting into trouble together. When I was running across rooftops or playing in the train yards, Gregory was always there with me. We went to

Memphis together every summer and we spent most weekends together in Chicago. We spent every Thanksgiving and Christmas together. I had graduated from high school and was on my way to college. Gregory had dropped out of high school and was on his way into the Army. Another chapter was about to unfold in my life, all because I had gone to a college fair and stopped by a booth. If the booth that I stopped in front of had been the University of San Francisco instead of Northeastern, I may have been flying westward instead of eastward.

The plane arrived in Boston and I took a taxi to the dormitory. I got out of the taxi and stood in Boston's cold winter air. My dormitory was several blocks from campus and a thousand miles away from the hopelessness and despair of Chicago's South Side. The street was quiet and there was nearly a foot of fresh snow. There were no police sirens. It was quiet and peaceful, and for the first time in a long time, I was at peace. Even though I did not know anyone in Boston, even though I did not have much money, even though I did not really know what to expect, I was ready to begin the journey toward discovering my dreams and myself. I took a deep breath and thought to myself, "Thank God. I am out of Chicago."

Sometimes, the journey toward your dreams will take you to places unimaginable.

The journey itself, can be as rewarding as the dream.

CHAPTER 11

College

It was January, 1975. In a few days, I was going to begin classes at Northeastern University, majoring in electrical engineering. After all, that is what Mr. Jones had told me to do. I took creative writing and poetry classes along with physics, calculus, chemistry, and statistics. It was not long before I discovered that being good in math and being smart was not good enough. Being good in high school only enables you to get into college. I was a long way from Du Sable High School and the south side of Chicago. There were a lot of people here and a lot of them were really smart. It seemed like all of them studied. All of the tables and chairs in the library and the study halls were filled with people every night. People sat around on the floors, studied in the lobbies of the dormitories or sat in empty classrooms. I can remember studying so hard that it felt as if my brain was going to explode. I would study until three o'clock in the morning and get back up at seven o'clock to make my first class at eight o'clock.

Growing up on the south side of Chicago, I thought that all African-American kids were poor and that most of them did not take school seriously. While there were not a lot of African-American students at Northeastern, there were a lot of African-American students attending colleges and universities throughout Boston. The ones who were there were smart and most of them were not poor. There were also African students from countries like Ghana, Nigeria, and Ethiopia. All of them were smart and none of them were poor! I got to know students at MIT, Harvard University, Boston College, Boston University, The Boston Conservatory of Music, Emerson College, Simmons College, Smith College, Radcliffe College, Babson College, Boston State, Tufts University, Wheelock College, and Wellesley College. A lot of the African-American students came from the East Coast—places like Philadelphia, New York, and Washington, D.C. I was the only student that I knew of from Chicago and I stood out like a sore thumb. My clothes were different and I talked differently. All of the East Coast students had eastern accents and talked really fast. I had a southern accent and I talked really slow. Not only that, but I had this huge Afro which I kept braided all the time and all of the guys from the East Coast had short hair cuts like the brothers from the Nation of Islam.

Eventually, I hooked up with Ronald Bell, Chuck Hughes, and Joe Myers. Ron and Joe were both from New York. Ron was from Staten Island and Joe was from Brooklyn. They were both engineering majors. Chuck was from Philadelphia and he was a marketing major. They helped me cut my Afro, lose my accent, come out of my platform shoes, and tone down my clothes. More importantly, they became the only friends that I had ever had who also had dreams and aspirations.

It was a good thing that I made friends, because nothing else was going right. My financial aid was in a perpetual state of disarray and the university threatened to hold up my registration every quarter. Fortunately, I had also made a friend in

Ernestine Whiting, the Director of Financial Aid. She took me on as her personal case. No matter what, she was determined that as long as I did not quit, she would not give up on me. Every quarter, for 5 years, she helped me find a way to pay my bills and register for school. My biggest problem was that there was so much pressure, I just could not keep up.

First, I dropped calculus. Then, I dropped chemistry and English composition. The first six months were a disaster. The time went by so fast that my head was spinning. I was studying harder than I had ever studied before, and I was falling further and further behind. All those days of clowning in class in elementary school; standing in the corridor in middle school; and sliding by in high school were all catching up with me.

Going to school at Northeastern was like trying out for the Du Sable High School football team. On the football team, we ran and ran until people dropped out. At Northeastern, we studied and studied until people dropped out. At Du Sable, we did sit-ups and push-ups until our stomachs and arms were sore and worn out. At Northeastern, we studied calculus, physics, and statistics until our brains were sore and worn out. The first day of practice at Du Sable, there were over 300 guys standing. On the first day of my chemistry class there were over 500 students standing. One by one, they began falling. I too, began to stumble and I almost fell.

I quickly and painfully discovered that bad habits are hard to break. If you have a habit of not studying until just before time to take the test, or turning assignments in late, or sitting in the back of the classroom and not paying attention, you will find it difficult to succeed in college. College is not like high school. The teachers do not beg you to pay attention. They do not accept late assignments. And, they do not mind failing you—period. They do not play. In my calculus class, the professor was from India. I was staying up so late studying, one day in class I just could not stay awake. Sitting in the front row, I fell asleep. The next thing I knew, he had thrown a piece of chalk at me. The chalk hit me on the head and I awoke to find the entire class staring at me. The professor was screaming at me with an Indian accent, "If you cannot stay awake in my classroom do not come back anymore!" It was not like middle school where the teacher put me out of class for a day. He was telling me that if I fell asleep again, I could not come back—EVER!

I discovered that I could not go through school being unprepared, being unorganized, being irresponsible, clowning around, making excuses, and then just turn it on and get serious! Your brain is like any other muscle in your body. You have to use it. You have to exercise it. You have to train and prepare it so that when it is time to apply yourself, your brain will be ready. You do not go out and run a 100-meter dash without stretching, training, preparing yourself mentally, and expect to win the race. I remembered back to high school when Coach Bonner ran us through the hallways, up the stairs, down the stairs, and back up again until some of the meanest, strongest, and toughest guys were falling out. Cigarettes and alcohol were catching up with them and their bodies could not compete. Being lazy all of those years in school was catching up with me and my brain just could not compete.

In my chemistry class, there were 500 students in a huge lecture hall. I had pages and pages of notes, and yet, I could not understand what was going on. I failed chemistry twice. Finally, I called my mama, in June, 1975. I told her I was going to come home. I was out of money. I had dropped out of most of my classes. I sat down and buried my head in my hands and I wondered, "Why am I studying engineering?"

Well, I did not go home. The more I thought about quitting college and going back to Chicago, the more I thought about how angry I was that they did not have a big celebration for the students who were going to college. I had also made myself a promise after I quit the football— I would never quit anything again in life.

As I sat there, I thought, "Maybe the reason they did not have a big celebration for all of the students who were going on to college was that they did not believe we would make it through college anyway." As I sat there, my mind kept going back to quitting the football team. I have always regretted the day I walked away from the football team. I wished I had someone to talk to, someone to share my fears with, and someone who would have just listened. I wished Coach Bonner had called me into his office and asked me what was wrong. I wished someone had asked me what my dreams were and helped me to understand how playing football could have become more than just surviving at Du Sable. If someone had taken the time to listen to me, perhaps they could have helped me to understand that I was good at football and that a football scholarship could help me get into college where I could major in journalism or literature. They could have exposed me to sports reporting, broadcast journalism, writing sports books or even sports photography. Perhaps they could have helped me to understand how I could have used the same courage, confidence, and determination that had helped me to make the team to pursue my dreams in life. Even though I did not have dreams of becoming a professional football player, the fact that I was strong enough to make the best football team in the city of Chicago was proof that I could achieve any dream. I wish I had someone like myself to talk to when I was fourteen years old. I would not have allowed me to quit!

Here I was, at another crossroads in my life. I could pack up and go back to Chicago or I could use that same determination that helped me to punch Reggie in the eye; the same determination that helped me survive at Du Sable High School; the same determination that helped me to survive the gangs and violence in Chicago; the same determination that helped me say no to drugs, alcohol, marijuana, and cigarettes when all of my friends were drinking, smoking, and getting high.

On this day, I had only myself to talk to. I was not going to allow myself to quit, but I was going to get out of the College of Engineering and forget about the advice I had received from Mr. Jones (even though I had not seen Mr. Jones since that day in his office).

I had the courage not to quit, however, my biggest problem was that I still had no one to talk to who could advise me of what to do next. My father worked for the Post Office. My mother was a seamstress. They did not know anything about becoming a writer or starting a publishing company. That is why I had been talking to Mr. Jones in the first place. Now that I was giving advice to myself, I could tell myself not to go backward, but I did not know how to tell myself to go forward. I did not say to myself, "You are in college, you want to be a writer, why not consider majoring in journalism or literature?" Since I had been lazy in school, I had not developed my brain muscles as strongly as I could have. With all of the studying I was now doing in college, I had probably popped a few thousand blood vessels in my brain. I still did not think about majoring in journalism, literature, marketing or education, all of which taught information and developed skills that I have come to rely upon now that I write and run a publishing company. Instead, I switched my major to business and computer science. I guess that by growing up poor, the idea of getting a well-paying job won out over the uncertainty of becoming a published author. I did not know any authors. I did not know anyone who owned a publishing company. None of my friends were majoring in journalism or had aspirations of becoming a writer. Nearly all of my friends were either in the college of engineering or in the college of business administration. Since engineering was out, business was in.

I went to the Dean of Students—Dean Roland Latham. He, like Ms. Whiting in financial aid, helped me to stay in school. Dean Latham helped me to transfer out of the College of Engineering and into the College of Business. That day in Dean Latham's office was another turning point in my life. I enjoyed the business classes much more than I had the engineering classes. I rose to the top of my class in accounting, statistics, and business policy. A year later, I reached another turning point.

One of the most prestigious co-op jobs for business majors was with the international public accounting and consulting firm of Arthur Andersen and Company. Each year, they only offered three or four jobs and they usually had nearly two hundred students to apply. I interviewed for one of the jobs and was bubbling with confidence with my 3.0 grade point average. I thought that a *B* average was "the bomb." After my interview, the College of Business notified me that I was not being offered a job. Forget being in college. My attitude went straight back to the ghetto. I called the managing partner at Arthur Andersen and Company with a major attitude, "Why didn't I get the job? I have a

3.0 grade point average. I have a recommendation from the Dean of Students. I want to know why I didn't get the job?"

Fortunately, the managing partner had a lot more sense than I did, and he calmly pointed out that most of the students who were inter-viewing for the job had 4.0 (straight A) grade point averages. However, since I was so sincerely interested in working for them, he would be willing to schedule another interview since they still had one more job to fill. I was so intent on getting that job I spent each of the next four days in the library researching the company. I knew everything about the company. Who their major clients were, how many people worked in the Boston office, where they had offices throughout the world, and that they were ranked the second largest public accounting firm in the world. I sailed through the interview and when the interview was over, the Managing Partner asked if I had any more questions, to which I responded, "Do I get the job?" He smiled and hired me on the spot. This was another turning point in my life. I realized that while my friends thought a *B* average was "the bomb" there were a lot of straight-A students, and they would always be competing for the best jobs and for the best opportunities. I decided that day that if *B's* were the bomb that I was going to be atomic, because straight *A's* were now my goal.

While I did not get straight *A's* every quarter, I began each quarter with a goal of getting straight *A's*. My "A" attitude transformed my thinking and my actions. I did not become arrogant but I exploded in self-confidence. I sat in the front of every class. I enrolled in the classes of the instructors with the reputation for being the hardest, several of whom wrote the textbooks. I joined study groups with the best students. My social circle expanded from all African-American students to whites, Latinos, Asians, Africans, Iranians, and anyone else interested in being the best. I began tutoring at the African-American Institute in accounting and statistics.

Everything was going great when I was called into the Dean of Students' office. I was told that I had fallen so far behind while I was in the college of engineering that it would be impossible for me to graduate with my class. It would take another full year for me to complete the number of credit hours needed to graduate. When I was told that there was no way I could accumulate enough credits to graduate with my class I thought about my father. His dream was to see me graduate from college and he expected to see me receive my degree in June, 1979, not in June, 1980. My father and mother had moved back to Memphis, Tennessee, while I was in college. My father had bought a house and fulfilled another of his dreams. I was not going to disappoint him and I was not going to watch Ron, Chuck, and Joe receive their degrees while I stayed at home. Besides, now I had my "A" game.

I left Dean Latham's office with focus and determination. When I first started at Northeastern, I was dropping 3 out of 4 classes while barely passing one class. Now, each quarter I began taking anywhere from 2 to 5 extra classes. The last quarter for me to qualify for graduation, I took nine classes and earned 8 *A's* and 1 *B,* and qualified to graduate with my class on time.

I went on to graduate with honors. I was one of the most respected students on campus. I was a math, statistics, and accounting tutor. I had organized the first graduation banquet at Northeastern University honoring African-American students. My mother and father boarded an airplane for the first time and flew to Boston for my graduation, the largest graduation ceremony of any university in Boston. The Northeastern University graduation was held at the Boston Garden, where the NBA's Boston *Celtics* played.

Dean Latham, Ms. Whiting, and my good friend, Harvette Emmett, who was the Assistant Director of the Northeastern University African-American Institute, helped me to discover how smart I really was. Ms. Emmett encouraged me to become a tutor and was always there to give me advice about school and about life. She became the big sister I never had and always found time to listen to my dreams and aspirations. She, Ms. Whiting, Dean Latham, other professors, family, and friends joined Ron, Chuck, Joe, and me at our apartment on graduation weekend. My father and mother, neither of whom had graduated from high school, stood in my apartment overlooking the Charles River, just a stone's throw away from the Harvard Business School, talking and laughing with Deans and professors. My journey had taken me a long way from the hopelessness of Pike County, Alabama, and the poverty of Chicago's South Side.

As they announced my name at the graduation ceremony, "Mychal Wynn" my mother and father sighed, "Thank you, Lord." I wondered what my second-grade teacher would have said?

In our home, college is not an option. When our children entered kindergarten, we intended for them to go to school until they graduate from college.

CHAPTER 12

I Have an Education, but What About My Dreams?

When I go to schools, I listen to students who believe that grades do not matter because no one is going to give them an opportunity anyway. I am glad that Mrs. Burke, Mr. Roberts, Ms. Emmett, Ms. Whiting, and Dean Latham helped me to understand that a lot of people want to help young people succeed. However, they also want to see students put forth some effort. Students should ask themselves the question, "Why should other people help me if I am not willing to help myself?" By graduating as one of the top students in my class and the student with the most improvement since that miserable first year of college, I had job offers from companies in Boston, Chicago, Atlanta, Miami, San Francisco, and San Jose, California. I was a long way from

Pike County, Alabama; and a long way from the south side of Chicago. Mr. Roberts was right, "If you think an education is expensive, try ignorance." I had an education that could provide me with opportunity. I was not looking for a job, jobs were looking for me. I had job offers from IBM, Arthur Andersen and Company, Coopers and Lybrand, and Ernst and Ernst. Most of the students whom I speak to have never heard of these companies, but for college students in 1979, these were some of the companies that everyone wanted to work for.

After flying all over the country, being treated to lunches and dinners, staying in hotels, ordering room service, and meeting with various corporate executives, I finally accepted a job as a Computer Systems Analyst with IBM. I was going to go to work at IBM's General Products Division in San Jose, California. At a starting salary of $35,000 per year (not including stock options), I was already making more than my father had made during the entire 33 years he had worked for the Postal Service. Within six months after arriving in San Jose, I bought a condo, a sports car, and filled my closet with clothes.

I was college educated, living in California, and driving along the coastline in a brand new sports car with the top down and the wind blowing in my face. I was a thousand miles from the violence of Chicago and a lifetime from the poverty of Pike County, Alabama. Yet, with all of this, I was not happy and I was not living my dream. I wanted to be a writer! While I was not rich, I could now understand how people who were rich could still be unhappy. Owning stuff and having money does not mean you are living your dream unless the stuff and the money were your only dreams to begin with. While I did not want to be poor, I never had the single dream of owning stuff. I never had a dream of making a lot of money. My dream was to become a writer and I was beginning to realize that I had gotten sidetracked.

I worked at IBM for two years. I had a manager whom I did not like and a job I could not stand. There was another job I really wanted in another computer programming area. However, to apply for that job, I would need to have a top-rated job evaluation from my current job. Here we go again, just like being back at Du Sable trying out for the football team. A lot of people were competing for a few positions—in this case, one job.

With the same attitude and determination that I used as a fourteen-year-old trying out for the football team, this became a matter of survival. At work, I stayed late and came in early. I did a great job and everyone knew I was doing a great job. If I had been in school I would have earned an A^{++}. I was doing extra credit. This went on for six months until it was time for my evaluation. The evaluation process at IBM was on a scale of 1-5 with 1 being the best. In fact, the rumor was that no one had ever received a 1. The highest evaluation that even the best people had received was a 2. That did not matter. I had exceeded all expectations for my job. I had earned a 1 and I expected a 1.

A funny thing happened in my manager's office. I forgot to take into account that this guy, sitting across the desk from me, had been with the company for nearly 30 years. His job was only two levels up from mine and I had only been with the company for two years. He sat behind his desk and told me how wonderful a job I had been doing and that he was pleased to give me a 3 evaluation. I said, "Excuse me?" He said, "Mychal, you've done a really good job and I think a 3 is a fair evaluation." *What's wrong with this picture?* I was expecting a 1 so I could get another job and he was giving me a 3, virtually ensuring that I would stay in this job for at least another year. Then I thought to myself, "He's already been here 30 years. I might be stuck here forever!"

I argued, but it did not do any good. When I was in school I liked to argue and debate with people. I always had my facts straight and I usually won the arguments, however, I was not in school and this was an argument I was not going to win, even though I had copies of reports that I had written and a list of all of the things I had accomplished. I asked for a review of the evaluation by the district vice president, but it did not do any good. I stayed around for another six months and something wonderful happened—I quit! However, unlike quitting the football team, a decision that I have always regretted, I have never regretted quitting my job at IBM. Do not get me wrong, IBM is a great company and there are a lot of good people who work for IBM. I still own stock in IBM. However, quitting my job there, more than any other decision I have made in life, helped me to discover my true dreams and opened the door to pursuing my passions.

The first dream I discovered was, I did not really want a job, I wanted to run my own business. It did not matter if I made a lot of money or not, I wanted to be in charge. The next dream I discovered was, not only did I love writing, but my passion is to write about things that will positively impact people's lives. I wanted my words to inspire and inform people.

I also discovered that my passion to argue my opinion has become a dream that has had an impact on a lot of lives. I have written and talked about how to improve schools and it has caused people to think about doing things differently. I do not want to see today's students become the hopeless, frustrated, and angry faces I saw on the street corners in Chicago when I was in school.

I also discovered I have a passion for working with young people and that young people listen to me. You may be reading this book because I spoke at your school. My two sons also listen to me, even though I am hard on them at times. I will not allow them to be lazy and I will not allow them to give up. They know I love them and I am passionate about helping them to discover their dreams.

The day I left my job at IBM was the day I truly discovered my dreams. I told my manager I was quitting and I told him where to send my final paycheck. I went down to the personnel office and signed a bunch of papers. I packed up my belongings, got into my sports car, went home, and called my mama.

"Hi mama, how are you doing?" My mother told me she was doing fine and asked, "So what's up son?" I responded, "I quit my job!" There was a long pause on the other end of the telephone. I thought that my mama had a heart attack. "Mama, mama, are you still there? Are you alright mama?" Finally, my mother said, "Son, why did you quit your job?" "I told Mr. Jones I wanted to be a writer. I'm going to be a writer mama," I answered. Upon hearing that, my mother said, "Boy! Couldn't you keep your job and write, too?"

My mother and I talked for a long time. For the first time in my life, I felt that she was actually listening to me. I know my mother could not tell me what to do to become a writer. She could not tell me how to start a publishing company. She just listened and I told her about all of my frustrations. I told her about my having never stopped writing poetry since the day I started back in the second grade. I must have talked to my mother for over three hours. She did not say much, she just listened. I had finally discovered my true dreams and I had finally convinced myself to follow my dreams. After I hung up the phone with my mother, I began making plans for the rest of my life. It did not matter how much money I would make. I had finally realized that doing what you love to do is more important than doing something you are unhappy doing because it pays a lot of money. However, I had not forgotten that being poor was no fun either. I was determined I would do what I loved to do, and I would figure out how to get paid for doing it.

I spent much of my life being afraid of failing. Now, I spend each day of my life fully confident about succeeding.

Change your attitude and change your outcomes.

Chapter 13

From Programmer to Poet

I left San Jose and moved to Los Angeles. I liked northern California, but there was something inside of me that was looking for a fresh start and a new beginning. It was as though leaving IBM, leaving my job to pursue my dream required a new beginning.

I had a good friend who was a computer programmer with whom I shared an apartment in an area of Los Angeles called Rancho Palos Verdes, an area of million dollar homes, which sat on a hillside overlooking Los Angeles. Rancho Palos Verdes was located just south of Los Angeles. As you drove down Hawthorne Boulevard to go into Los Angeles, you could see the entire city. As I turned the corner each day to drive to the University of Southern California, where I did my research on writing and publishing, I looked out over the city of Los Angeles and I knew if I could make it out of the south side of Chicago, I could eventually make it as a writer.

I had gone to school from kindergarten through the twelfth grade. I had spent 5 years in college where I had graduated with honors. I knew how to write computer programs, how to buy a house, and how to invest in stocks. I knew about economics, calculus, physics, statistics, accounting, and all sorts of other things. Yet, I did not know anything about how to follow my dreams.

I spent nearly every day of my first six months in Los Angeles at the library. I found myself reading more books than I had ever read while attending school, and I was writing. I was writing poetry. I was writing letters to companies requesting information. I was writing marketing strategies. I was writing brochures. I was writing flyers. The librarian became my best friend. Every morning, I was there when the library opened and I was asking her to direct me to the books on writing, publishing, and starting a business. I had a passion for writing since the second grade, but there was nothing in school that had prepared me to become a professional writer or build a publishing company. I had taken English grammar, which helped me to speak. I had taken math and science, which helped me to think. I had taken calculus, physics, statistics, chemistry, social studies and a bunch of other stuff. However, I had not written a single research paper on becoming a writer or on starting a publishing company. Now, I was doing more reading, research, and writing than ever. It was not because I was trying to get a grade or to impress a teacher; I was following my dreams. I needed to know everything I could to help me to become a successful writer and to build a business.

Each day, my roommate got up to go to work and I got up to go to the library. I was discovering a passion within myself, one which I believe all people have. We all have passions deep within us, whether it is getting up early to play a video game, determined to overcome whatever obstacles to reach the next level; whether it is a political campaign or environmental concern which causes someone to stay up late and get up early to let his or her voice be heard; whether it is the kid who goes out to the basketball court in the snow and ice to practice a jump shot; whether it is the school teacher who reads books, talks to other teachers and parents, takes classes, and does research with a determination to make the connection with one student who does not appear to be motivated to learn.

I reflected on my years in middle school when I would get tired and fall asleep after reading a few pages from a book or when I would study for an hour and feel that my head was about to explode. Now, I was going to the library when it opened and I was staying until closing. I did not think about eating or drinking. I was consumed with discovering how to become a successful writer and how to build a publishing company. This, in itself, was a significant choice with significant consequences.

If I had chosen to concentrate solely on writing, I could have written a lot more than the twenty books that I have so far. As a writer, your responsibilities are simple. You create a manuscript and give it to an agent who presents it to a publisher. You negotiate a contract with the publisher and you begin working on your next book.

However, if you choose to become a writer AND a publisher, as I did, then writing the book is only the beginning of a long, involved, and expensive process. Going to college helped to prepare me for this in ways unimaginable when I was at Du Sable High School. My college classes in accounting, marketing, statistics, and English composition helped me to understand some of the complexities of running a business—inventory management, pricing, break-even analysis, marketing, promotions, customer relations, advertising, and financial management. I was now involved in learning about the business of publishing and the art of writing. I also learned how to manage my time, develop my speaking and presentation skills, do research, write reports, plan, and think.

Most of the people whom I have met who want to become a writer or a speaker have not developed the passion required to make it happen. I meet people who say they want to become a writer. I share with them the details about how I got started. I tell them the books they need to read, the research they need to do, and the steps that they need to take. Yet, very few people move beyond talking about their dreams to actually following their dreams. I have bumped into people years after they asked me what they needed to do to follow their dreams of writing and they have not read any of the books, done any of the research, or done any of the work. They are still just talking about doing it.

As I talk to people about the types of things I did and the type of things they must do to seriously pursue their dreams, I can tell if they truly have a dream or if they simply have a wish. I believe that your dreams evolve from your passions and that you are willing to put forth the effort and do the work necessary to achieve the dream. However, if it is a wish, then you talk about it as if it were a dream, but what you are really saying is that you "wish" you could go into a particular career. The young lady at Washington High School who said she wanted to become a doctor had a "wish." She had not put forth any of the effort required to turn the wish into a reality. It was not really her dream. In fact, most students whom I meet in schools "wish" they could become doctors, lawyers, athletes or entertainers. Every now and then their dreams truly represent their passions. However, most often, they are just wishes. Students think these professions make a lot of money, so they "wish" they could go into one of these professions. Usually, they have not done any research and do not know anything beyond what they have seen on television. Their grades and study habits are not consistent with becoming successful in any of these careers.

I have found that people who wish for things can always find reasons why their wishes will not come true. They do not make a commitment to themselves to do the work, gain the knowledge, make the contacts or expose themselves to the people and circumstances that will help them to become successful. And, they spend a lot of time complaining or making excuses.

People who have dreams, which evolve from their passions, will start early and stay late. They will talk to people and do research. They will try and fail and try again. They will stumble and fall, gather their strength, and get up again. I did not have a wish of becoming a writer, I had a *dream* of becoming a writer. I did not wish I could start a publishing company, I was *committed* to starting a publishing company as a means of pursuing my dream of becoming a writer. Rather than sitting around "wishing" for a publishing company to publish my books, I was going to start my own publishing and publish my own books. That is how I was going to make my dream a reality!

Whenever I was not writing poetry, I was researching how to get published and how to start a publishing company. After about six months, I knew a lot about the publishing business, but, I was running out of money. My final paycheck from IBM was spent a long time ago, and my savings had gone bone dry. I took the last money I had and printed 24 of my poems onto greeting cards and posters. I went to the California Mart where I met sales reps who were responsible for selling greeting cards to card stores, grocery stores, gift shops, and all of the places where there are greeting card racks and displays. I had a portfolio of all of my cards and I had sales and marketing sheets outlining my sales and marketing strategies. I identified the places where my cards could be sold and the types of people who would purchase them.

I had done my research and I had put all of my college education to use. However, no one would help me. They said my verses were inspiring, but other companies had similar types of cards. They gave me reason after reason why my cards would not sell. No matter how many people told me that they would not help me, I never got discouraged and I never considered quitting. My attitude was, "If you are not going to help me sell my cards, then I will sell them myself."

I spent the last of my money and some of my friend's money on printing 24 verses onto greeting cards, posters, and T-shirts. I stuck an eight-foot table into the back of my sports car, along with my cards, posters, and T-shirts. I got up each Friday, Saturday, and Sunday morning at 5:00 a.m. and went out to the boardwalk at Venice Beach. I paid $50 a day for a ten-foot space. I set up a table and I began living my dream. I was a writer and I owned my own publishing company. I was doing what I wanted to do and I was getting paid to do it. I just was not getting paid a lot.

I eventually moved out of the apartment that I shared with my friend into my own apartment. My new apartment did not have any furniture. It was a production facility. I silk-screened T-shirts in the bathroom. I was soon putting my poetry onto wooden plaques that I made in the living room. I wrote poetry in the bedroom and I stored my inventory everywhere. I had cards, posters, plaques, and T-shirts all over the place. I eventually bought a used van and I had stuff all over my apartment and stuffed into my van.

Following your dreams does not guarantee that you will succeed quickly, if at all. In my situation, I had to accept that not everyone liked my poetry or thought enough of it to pay for it.

When I began selling my poetry on greeting cards, posters, and T-shirts along the boardwalk at Venice Beach, California, I was standing there one day when a group of young ladies stopped at my table. One of the young ladies began reading one of my posters. It was a poem entitled, *If You Are My Friend.*

If You Are My Friend ...

If you are my friend
    be honest with me
    even if it hurts

If you are my friend
    push me forward
    when I want to quit

If you are my friend
    acknowledge my faults
    and help me to correct them

If you are my friend
    be critical of me
    when I am not critical of myself

If you are my friend
    I can turn to you
    during difficult times

If you are my friend
    I can cry around you
    and not be ashamed

If you are my friend
    I can share my feelings
    and not offend you

If you are my friend
    all these things I will do for you

        — Mychal Wynn

As the young lady leaned over my table and read the poem a tear fell from her eye. She looked up and asked, "You wrote this?" I stood there with pride (thinking to myself, "Yeah, I'm bad") as I responded, "Yes. My name is Mychal Wynn."

She went on to ask, "Is this for sale?"

"Yes."

"How much is it?"

"The posters are only two dollars each."

She pushed the poster back across the table toward me and said, "For a piece of paper?"

With that, she and her two girlfriends started laughing and walked away. They went to the next table and bought some cheap earrings, 3 for $5.00, and then strutted back past me to the table on the other side and bought some cheap T-shirts, 3 for $10.00!

There I stood with my dream on the table, my heart, soul, and deepest emotions written into a verse that had caused her to shed a tear and she stood there and implied that my poetry, my heart, my soul, was not worth $2.00?

So what! I did not allow that to stop me and it is a good thing I did not quit, because now I sell thousands of posters, and that one, *If You Are My Friend*, has been one of my best selling posters for 18 years. You cannot give up, even if no one else thinks that your dream is important.

Following your dreams does not guarantee that you will succeed. However, not following your dreams will guarantee that you have no chance of succeeding.

CHAPTER 14

Living My Dream

I was soon selling my poetry all over the country. I drove from Los Angeles to places as far away as New York City and Miami, Florida. Sometimes I would drive from Los Angeles to Memphis. I would drive along Interstate 40 through Nevada, Arizona, New Mexico, Oklahoma, Texas, and Arkansas. I would spend a couple of days with my parents in Memphis, Tennessee, telling them about all of the places that I was going and how my publishing company was growing. As I talked about my dreams, my father got so excited that he asked to come with me on some of my trips.

When I was growing up, my father and I did not talk a lot. We would watch Friday-night boxing together, but we never really talked. Now, here I was, riding with my father for hours and we talked about everything. It was like riding with a person whom I was just meeting for the first time. Since my father always dreamed of driving a big 18-wheeler, I would always let him drive (even though it was only a van). He would talk on the CB radio to the truckers. My father usually rode with me on trips that would take me from Memphis up through Chicago.

We would drive to Chicago and he would stay with my aunt. I would drive on to the city where I was going to sell my things. Sometimes it was Detroit, Michigan; Gary, Indiana; or other cities in the area. This was really a lot of fun and my father was proud that I was following my dream and that I was building my company.

I continued driving all over the country selling my poetry on greeting cards, plaques, posters, and T-shirts. I sold them at art shows, conferences, on college campuses, and by mail. Before long, I was reciting poetry at churches, banquets, and on various programs. People and organizations began paying me to write special poems. I wrote a poem entitled, *What Manner of Woman*, for a family reunion tribute to a good friend's great aunt. I wrote a poem called, *Children We Care*, for the California Foster Parent Association. I also wrote verses and published cards for sororities and other organizations.

As my publishing company grew, I was being invited to speak and to read poetry at schools and organizations all over the country. I was living my dream, traveling, meeting a lot of people, and having a lot of fun. That is when my dream changed.

Whenever you follow your dreams, there are seeds that are planted along the way that sprout into new dreams. Before you know it, you will have sown a garden of dreams.

Chapter 15

Dreams Change

The thing that I have learned about following your dreams is that they keep growing and they keep changing. As you work toward achieving your dreams, you meet new people, get knew ideas, are exposed to new information, and gain new experiences. You learn more and do more. The more you learn, the more you want to learn. The more you do, the more you want to do. As you achieve one dream, you develop two, three, four or five others. Each time you achieve one of your dreams, you begin to dream even greater dreams. In the process of working toward and achieving your dreams, you meet more people who inspire you on toward even greater dreams.

All of my closest friends have dreams and they inspire me toward achieving even greater dreams. My friends and I sit around and share our dreams and we have some dreams in common. My friend,

Alphonso Carreker, played college football at Florida State University and thirteen years of professional football for the Denver Broncos and the Green Bay Packers. He and I dream of developing a special program for students who are interested in learning about the business of professional football. My friend, Greg Jones, is an executive with the Oracle Corporation, the largest Internet software company in the world. He and I talk about dreams of spending time together with our families, sailing on a houseboat or spending time at their lake house in the summers. My friend, Jean Polyne, is an engineer with the General Electric Company. He and I talk about our dreams for our children. He has a daughter who is the age of my older son and a son the same age as my younger son. We talk about their futures, the colleges they will attend, and about how to help them discover their dreams. My friend, Greg Williams, sells Rolls Royces. He and I talk about the dreams that he has for his daughter, currently attending high school, and the colleges that he would like for her to be accepted into. I talk to him about my dream of one day owning a Rolls Royce or Bentley!

Many of the teachers and principals whom I work with have dreams of writing books or of telling stories about how they have changed their schools from low-performing to high-performing schools. I am always working with teachers and principals who discuss their dreams and the books they are interested in writing or publishing. I have already co-authored a book with Dee Blassie, entitled, *Building Dreams: K-8 Teacher's Guide*. This all came about after Dee, an elementary school teacher, wrote me a letter after hearing me talk about helping students to discover and to pursue their dreams. She wanted to become a part of my "Dream Team" and she wanted to do all of the things that I had talked about in her classroom with her students and their parents. Dee's friend, Dr. Peggy Dolan, a former elementary school principal, who developed a program in her school that helped students to learn how to resolve conflicts without fighting or name-calling. I worked with her to realize her dream of publishing a book entitled, *Fight-Free Schools: Creating a school culture that nurtures achievement*.

In 1985, my dreams were forever changed the day that I was invited to work with a group of seventh- and eighth-grade students at Forshay Jr. High School in Los Angeles. I was asked to work with a group of students who had bad attitudes. I was to teach them how to write and recite poetry. While working with them, I was to talk to them about their dreams and about their attitudes. When they walked into the room on that first day, pants sagging, hair uncombed, and with major attitudes, I just shook my head. When I looked at them, I saw myself back at Corpus Christi. I remembered how uninspired I was and how much trouble I had caused. That first day, I told them about my dreams and about my life. I told them that if they were willing to make a commitment to work with me, I would help them to discover their dreams.

We worked together every morning for three weeks, talking about and reciting poetry. As we worked together, we talked, we wrote and recited poetry, and we eventually developed a goal of presenting a poetry recital in an assembly before the entire school. By the time we were done, they had been transformed! The young men walked and spoke like young men who were going someplace in life. The young ladies walked and spoke like young ladies who were destined to become doctors, lawyers, teachers or television commentators. When we presented the assembly, they blew everyone away! They were awesome. They learned that if you can recite a poem with passion in front of 800 of your friends and captivate them to the point of being able to hear a pin drop, you can do anything. As I sat in the assembly listening to their friends, "Yo man, look at Ronnie. I didn't know he could talk like that," I remembered Mr. Roberts and folk dancing at Edmund Burke Elementary School. He knew that we probably were not going to grow up and pursue a career in folk dancing. However, he wanted us to experience success. Many of these students did not have dreams of growing up to become writers, poets or speakers. However, they were experiencing success.

As I walked through the corridors of their school, I saw young people with tremendous potential, many of them dragging, pants sagging, with broken spirits and shattered dreams. I remembered my second-grade teacher, "I doubt if he will ever make it out of elementary school." From that day, I developed the dream of turning every school into a place of passion and purpose, a place where students want to learn and where teachers want to teach. Since that day, I have worked with over five hundred thousand parents, teachers, and students in schools throughout America and in other countries. With the same passion with which I pursued writing and publishing, I have done research, talked to the best principals and teachers, worked hands-on with parents and students, identified the types of things that the best schools are doing, and developed plans about how to improve any school. When schools are unable or unwilling to change, I have written books to help parents and students plan how to get into college in spite of their school.

Everything that I have learned, I have used as a parent with my own children. My wife and I have helped them to understand how they learn, how they are smart, and where their passions are. We have helped them to understand how to become good students and we have worked with their teachers to ensure that they become the best students they are capable of becoming.

Working with those seventh- and eighth-grade students at Forshay Junior High School changed my life in a way that they will probably never know. They inspired within me even greater dreams, one of which was to become the best father I could be. As they inspired me, I want to inspire you to discover your dreams. I want to inspire your teachers to help you to understand how what they are teaching can help you to achieve your dreams. And, I want to inspire your parents to nurture your dreams. Ask your parents and teachers if they will become part of your *Dream Team.*

While I do not know what happened to all of those students, I did hear one of the young ladies speak at a banquet several years later, attended by many prominent people in Los Angeles. In the audience was Tom Bradley, the mayor of Los Angeles, along with other politicians and local business people. The young lady was a senior in high school and about to go to college with dreams of becoming a lawyer. She stepped up to the podium as a stately and beautiful young woman. She was a long way from the smart mouth, bad attitude, sassy young woman whom I had met as a seventh-grader. She politely thanked everyone for coming and for the invitation to share her thoughts. She then raised her voice and spoke brilliantly for nearly an hour. She inspired and captivated everyone in the room, just as she and the other students had captivated their friends by reciting poetry in their middle school assembly. She was a confirmation that I was doing the right thing and that my dreams had led me in the right direction.

> *You cannot predict where your dreams will lead you, the people they will introduce you to or ultimately the impact you will have on the world. It will require all of your courage to pursue so many unknowns.*

CHAPTER 16

Courage

Discovering your dreams is one thing, pursuing your dreams is something different. Many people will talk about their dreams, however, few people will actually get up and begin working toward achieving their dreams. I do not believe it is because people are lazy. I believe it is because they are afraid. Overcoming your fear of failure is the first step toward achieving your dreams. There is no guarantee that all of the hard work, all of the studying, all of the time and money you invest in pursuing your dreams will result in success. You have to be willing to fail before you can begin to succeed.

I have failed hundreds of times. Things I thought would work, did not. Speeches I thought would be inspiring, were not. Cards, posters, and books I thought would become best sellers, hardly sold any at all. Business partnerships I thought would work, failed miserably. People who I thought would support me, did nothing but try to stop me from succeeding. Yet, in spite of it all, I have never had a pity party. I have never whined, complained or wondered, "Why do these things happen to me?" I have never complained about being adopted, being black, being discriminated against, being poor or anything else. Complaining is a waste of time and a waste of energy. Focusing on what is not working distracts you from thinking about what might work.

Continuing without complaining leads you into the paths of people who will encourage, support, and even inspire you. When I began publishing my poetry, I never envisioned myself writing a book. I had only planned to publish greeting cards, posters, and plaques with my inspirational verses. One day, at an art show, a very kindly older lady, who reminded me of my grandmother, came to my table and read every verse. She smiled and told me that I had wisdom beyond my years, "For such a young man, there is so much wisdom within your words. Have you ever thought of putting your verses into a book?" She and I talked for a while and she purchased one of everything I had written. That night, I kept replaying her words over and over in my mind, *"Have you ever thought of putting your verses into a book?"* From that conversation, I was inspired to publish my first book of poetry. From that first book of poetry, I have written 20 other books, none of which I had ever imagined I would write. As I reflect over all of the years I have been writing, I can remember many people like that lady who have encouraged and supported me. There have been pastors, teachers, principals, superintendents, students, friends, family, and countless other people who have come into my life and inspired me as much as I have inspired others through my writings. In fact, this book was inspired by a seventh-grader who asked, "Mr. Wynn when are you going to write a book about how you discovered your dreams?" I could not have done this alone, and yet, none of these people could have helped me if I had not had the courage to pursue my dreams.

I still meet people who knew me when I was a young, starving poet with a dream. They remember my journey, which began alone. Later, they saw me with my girlfriend (who became my wife). Then later, with my wife. A year later, they saw my wife and me with our son in a stroller. Years later, my wife and son were helping me, while his younger brother had taken over his spot in the stroller. Recently, in Philadelphia, my older son (now in college) worked with me for a week at a conference. Throughout the conference, people kept telling him about how they had known me when I first started, and how they remembered him in a stroller.

It was the pursuit of my dreams that allowed me to meet my wife, Nina. After about three years of struggling along; driving around the country; going to art shows, street fairs, schools, college campuses, and conferences; all of the prestige of working for IBM was gone. I no longer had credit cards. I no longer owned a home. I no longer had a sports car. I did not have any stocks, bonds or money in the bank. All I had was my dream, my writings, and my old van. Most people who knew I had left the security and prestige of working at IBM for such an insecure and unpretentious life as a poet, thought I had lost my mind. I had gone from designer suits to shorts and T-shirts. I had gone from a sports car to an old Ford van. I had gone from owning a fully furnished, $200,000 home in the Silicon Valley (worth about 1.5 million dollars today), to an apartment, furnished with milk crates.

I was selling my poetry at a conference in San Diego, California. After the conference was over, I went to the hotel restaurant to get a sandwich (that is about all I could afford). I was sitting there eating and watching television when a woman walked in and stood right between the television and me. "Excuse me," I said. She did not pay me any attention, "Excuse me!" I said again. She turned around and said, "Are you talking to me?" I said, "Yes, you're standing in front of the television." She said, "I'm sorry, I am supposed to meet my friends here, and I don't see them." So do you know what I did? I asked her to sit with me until her friends came.

At first she said she would just walk around and look for her friends, but I said, "If they come in, you can see them from here. They will have to walk right by us." Nina shrugged her shoulders, "I guess you're right," and sat down. Nina and I talked and talked. I told her why I was at the hotel and about my dream of writing and about how I had left IBM.

Finally, her friends came, but we continued talking. Three hours later, Nina took me for a drive along the San Diego shoreline. We got out and walked along the beach. I continued telling her about my dreams and all of the things I had been doing since leaving IBM. She told me about her job at TRW and what she did. She told me about how much she admired someone who had the courage to follow his dreams, and she began talking about her dreams of owning her own business and of buying a home.

It was almost sunrise by the time we finished talking. Nina drove me back to the hotel. I got out of her car and walked into the hotel lobby. I did not tell her that I could not afford a room, so I walked through the hotel lobby to the parking lot in the back where I was sleeping in my van!

After I left San Diego, I sent Nina one of the greeting cards I had written. Actually, I sent her a different card every day for two weeks. She has kept my poems all of these years (and that was over 20 years ago). Nina was the woman whom

I had dreamed of marrying. She did not care that I was struggling when she met me. She did not care that I did not own anything but an old van and my cards and posters. She would go with me on weekends to help me sell my things at art shows. She even took off from work to go with me to Seattle, Washington, and on another trip to Miami, Florida. Her friends thought she was crazy to "waste her time with some fool peddling his stuff all over the country." She had a sports car, a beautiful apartment, a highly paying job, credit cards, and stocks. They often asked her, "Why do you want to hook up with some guy who writes poetry?"

Nina believed in me because I believed in myself. She saw me get up early, stay up late, and never complain. She stood with me and stood by me and we fell in love. Two years later we were married.

Nina left her job at TRW to join me in my dream. She is now President and CEO of Rising Sun Publishing (that is our company). Even though my wife and I own all of the stock in Rising Sun Publishing, since she is the President and CEO, technically, I work for her. I had never thought of it in this way until recently. After speaking with a group of students at a middle school in South Carolina, upon hearing me talk about my wife, a young lady raised her hand. "Excuse me, Mr. Wynn. If Mrs. Wynn is the President and CEO of Rising Sun Publishing, then don't you work for her?" I had not thought of it in that way before, but I guess that if I am going to work for anyone, I could not think of a better person to work for than my wife.

Nina has been a dream wife, dream mother, and dream business partner. She has her own dreams and she works everyday to help our children and all children discover their dreams. I guess her friends were right, she was crazy. She was crazy enough to overcome her fears and to have the courage to leave her job as I had left mine. She was also crazy enough to have the faith that we could work together to pursue our dreams.

Following our dreams has been hard work; much harder than having a job where we go to work at nine o'clock and get off at five o'clock. Nina usually starts her day at 5:00 a.m. Now that our older son has gone off to college, she gets our younger son ready for school, runs our office all day, helps our son with his homework, checks her e-mail (particularly for e-mail from our son's teachers), and prepares to do it all over again the next day. She spends all day on the telephone with superintendents, principals, bookstores, and other people who want me to speak at their schools or for their organizations. Nina works all day in our business, works before and after work with our son, runs our household, and still finds time to go to the gym to work out.

We have built Rising Sun Publishing together. She joined me in support of my dream, and now, it has become our dream. Each day, we are helping others to develop the courage to follow their dreams. Nina gets letters from teachers, parents, and students about how our books and programs have inspired them to pursue their dreams. She has helped her administrative assistant to discover her dreams. When Nina met Shannon, she had dropped out of school, was out of work, and was wasting each day sitting in front of her house doing nothing. Nina inspired her, hired her, and became her friend. Shannon learned how to operate a computer, manage an office, and is growing each day by discovering her own dreams.

Many of the students whom I talk to in schools who are not doing well in their classes are not dumb or lazy or unable to do the work. They just do not have the courage to try because of their fear of failing. When called upon to read in class, students who have difficulty reading often clown around or otherwise misbehave in class because they are afraid of people laughing at them. Other students, who want to join a particular club, team, or activity do not join because they are afraid of being rejected, or of their friends talking about them. It is the fear of failing that keeps people from ever getting started. The fear of rejection keeps people from meeting and getting to know others. I am glad I was not afraid to pursue my dream and I am glad I was not afraid to meet Nina.

When you try something, there is no guarantee you will succeed. However, if you are afraid to try, then you are guaranteed you cannot succeed.

The greatest of all moral values is courage. People who have the courage to try, the courage to stand up for what is right and just, the courage to do the right thing because it is the right thing to do, will one day shape a world that, today, we can only dream of.

CHAPTER 17

You Must Have a Plan

On September 13, 1987, Nina and I got married. This was the second time my mama and daddy boarded an airplane. The first time, they were flying from Chicago to Boston to attend my graduation from college. Now, they were flying from Memphis to Los Angeles to attend my wedding. Nina and I had a lot of friends in Los Angeles and Nina has a lot of family. We had a big wedding at the Lakewood Country Club. It was a dream wedding. We had a buffet set up with all of the food you could eat. The wedding was outside in the warm California sun. Nina was so beautiful. This, too, was a long way from Chicago's South Side.

A few months before Nina and I got married, I had an important decision to make. While I owned a store, I was not making enough money to support a family. All of the work I was doing with teachers and students was volunteer work, so I was not getting paid at all. Now, I needed to develop a new plan.

Nina and I talked and I decided I was going to go back to work. I stopped working with the schools and continued my research and writing in the evenings or whenever I could find time. Even though I had said I never wanted to work for anyone again after I left IBM, I was excited about getting a job because I had a plan. I was going to get a job and work for five years. Over that period of time, I would save money, develop a line of credit, and buy property so that I could continue building our publishing company. *Why 5 years?* Because with many companies, you can buy stock in the company at a discounted price, but they will not allow you to keep it all unless you have worked for the company for a certain amount of time. With most companies, that amount of time is five years. This is called being fully vested in the stock plan. Remember what I said about gaining KNOWLEDGE? If it sounds a little confusing, do not worry. I had the knowledge that I needed to help me to develop my plan. This is another good reason to pay attention in school. While they may not teach you about stock plans in school, they do teach you how to think and how to do math. Pay attention!

Now that I had a plan, I had many choices to make. Where would I get a job? How much money would I ask for as a salary? How would I convince a company that I was serious about going back to work after working for myself for nearly five years? One of the choices I had was, while I was trying to find a full-time job I still needed to get started making more money so Nina and I could save for our wedding.

From 10:30 p.m. to 2:30 a.m., I worked at United Parcel Service unloading trucks.

From 9:00 a.m. to 5:00 p.m., I worked for a temporary agency doing word processing.

From 6:00 p.m. to 9:00 p.m., I worked at the Macy's department store selling men's clothes.

I know it sounds crazy, but remember what I said about having a passion. I was determined I was going to successfully build a publishing company and a family. I had a plan.

For me to do this, I had to swallow my pride. Although I had a college degree, I was slinging boxes at UPS for $8.50 an hour. I was making nearly $50,000 a year before I left IBM. I still owned my own business. I was a published author, and here I was in a truck with high school and college kids, slinging boxes. Just like at IBM, I had a supervisor whom I did not like. In fact, my supervisor at UPS did not like me, either. On my first evaluation he wrote, "Mychal lacks initiative!" I was working three jobs, writing, building a publishing company in my free time, planning a wedding, and he thought I lacked initiative? Go figure.

I continued slinging boxes, doing word processing, and selling men's clothing until I got a job at the Transamerica Corporation designing computer software. My starting salary was $30,000 a year. With stock options and bonuses, I had doubled my salary to $60,000 a year by the last year of my five-year plan. I had also accumulated nearly $30,000 worth of Transamerica stock. Now this is nothing like the millions of dollars in stock options that some people earned at the "dot-com" companies. Keep in mind that you cannot concern yourself with what other people are doing. You have to develop your own plan. You have to follow your own dream.

Nina and I continued building our publishing company and I continuing working at Transamerica. A year after we were married, we had our first son. Four years later, right in line with my plan, Nina left her job at TRW and I left my job at Transamerica. Our business had grown so much and I was traveling so often that we decided to move to a part of the country where traveling would not be so difficult. Most of the school districts that were inviting me to work with their teachers and students were in the Midwest and the southeastern part of the country, in states like Florida, South Carolina, North Carolina, Ohio, and Kentucky.

Nina and I considered Dallas, Texas; Cincinnati, Ohio; and Atlanta, Georgia. We decided to relocate to the Atlanta area. We rented our house in California and bought a home in Marietta, Georgia, just outside of Atlanta. We wanted a home big enough for our business. We needed a house with enough space to store our books and materials and large enough for Nina and I to both have offices. We considered office space, but after getting up to go to work at TRW for over twenty years, Nina did not want to get up, get dressed, and waste an hour in traffic to get to her own business. Her dream was to run her company from home, where she could wake up, have a cup of coffee, and start working.

Just as we had a sense of determination in everything else we had done together, Nina and I were determined to find our dream house. Remember when I told you that when you are serious about following your dream you meet people who will help you? It is as if you attract people who have positive attitudes and who will support and encourage you. Our real estate agent, Toni Rainsford, was such a person. We shared our story with her and told her about our dream house. Toni was determined to work with Nina until the dream was realized.

In June, 1992, Nina and Toni began looking at houses from Peachtree City, Georgia, 45 minutes south of Atlanta, to Alpharetta, Georgia, 30 minutes north of Atlanta. They looked all over

Atlanta and everywhere in between. By the time they were done, they had looked at over 500 houses. Finally, in Marietta, we found our dream home. In an area called East Cobb, one of the most prestigious communities and with some of the best public schools in Georgia, we bought a 5,500 square foot, 6 bedroom, 4 bathroom home, on one and a half acres of land, with a swimming pool, and surrounded by beautiful flowers and trees. Nina had an office upstairs and my office was downstairs. The school bus stopped at the bottom of our driveway and our son's school was just around the corner. Our publishing company was growing and we were living the life of our dreams.

A year after moving to Atlanta, Nina and I went to Africa. I was working on a book about African and African-American history and we traveled to Egypt and Ghana. This, too, was a dream come true. We had both wanted to visit Africa to study our history. We spent time in the Egyptian cities of Cairo, Luxor, and Aswan. We sailed along the Nile River, visited the Great Pyramids, rode camels, visited the great temples and tombs in the Valley of the Kings, and visited the great

Nubian temples in Abu Simbel. We also spent time in Ghana where we went from the capital city of Accra to the coast where we visited the slave dungeons. We walked where our ancestors had walked as they were taken off the African continent through the "Door of No Return" on their journey to the Americas. Seven months after returning from Africa we had our second son, Jalani Malik Wynn.

Nina was an athlete when she was growing up. She ran track, and played basketball, volleyball, and baseball. She loved sports, however, no one ever encouraged her to pursue her passion in sports, so she eventually stopped competing. Ever since I have known my wife, she has always taken care of herself and worked out. But once she stopped working for someone else and started running her own business, she began making time to really take care of herself. She joined a health club, worked out on weights, and took aerobics classes every day. While I loved playing basketball, I hated working out, but here we go again with this dream thing. When you have a passion for something, you inspire people around you. Nina inspired me to work out with her and even take aerobics classes. Each morning after the school bus picked up Mychal-David, we dropped Jalani off at preschool, and headed to the health club.

A new dream was developing—a husband and wife running their business together and working out together. Nina was having so much fun that she just got carried away. Her dreams were beginning to explode. One day while sharing her passion for sports and working out with one of the aerobics instructors, Cess, the instructor, told Nina she was going to be competing in a body-building competition and suggested that Nina meet her trainer. Cess introduced Nina to Basil, her trainer, and Nina developed a new dream. To compete in a bodybuilding competition!

Basil and his brother Fadi were both from Lebanon. They were both bodybuilders. They had started in high school. While Basil only trained others to compete, Fadi, himself, had won several competitions. They both were experts at muscular development and nutrition. Remember what I said about knowledge? *What you know will eventually determine what you get paid.* Basil had the knowledge and people were willing to pay for it. Basil was an expert at diet, nutrition, muscular development, and proper training techniques. Although he had not graduated from college and did not have a degree in nutrition or physical education, he was earning $90-per-hour training people like Nina.

Nina began training with Basil. She worked hard and she got stronger and stronger. She looked better than she did when we got married, and she was beautiful then. People often think that female bodybuilders look masculine. This is not true. While there are some women who develop such large muscle mass that they begin to look masculine, there are a lot of women who develop what they call "lines and cuts" that define the physique without developing big muscles. That was Nina. She had muscles popping out that I had never seen before. She was looking goooooooood!

Nina was just about ready to enter a competition when something happened to distract her from her dream. In March, 1997, Nina and I had been working out together. I was lifting weights and I accidentally bumped my elbow. I already had a sore on my elbow from a spider bite. When I hit my elbow with the weights, the sore began to bleed. It really hurt, but I washed it off and did not think anything else about it. The next morning I put on a Band-Aid and flew to California to speak to teachers in Pasadena and Los Angeles. What I did not know was that I had caused the spider bite to become infected with both strep and staph bacteria. The next day, after flying to California, I went into the hospital. Over the next 29 days I had a heart attack, a stroke, kidney failure, and developed a blood clot in my heart. I spent most of that time in intensive care clinging to life.

The fifteen doctors working on my case thought that I might not make it. My body had gone into septic shock and they did not know whether or not they could stop the infection. All of our dreams were falling apart. With me in the hospital over 2,000 miles away, Nina could not concentrate on her training. Over the next 29 days in the hospital, I made it through, but my body was frail and weak. I lost over 25 pounds and the doctors thought I would never be able to fully use my arm again. Because of the blood clot in my heart, the doctors said I could not fly on an airplane. When I got out of the hospital, Nina had to drive to California to get me and drive me back to Georgia. I wrote a book about that time in my life entitled, *Test of Faith*. It was weeks before I could work out again and over a year before my body completely healed. Before I went into the hospital, Nina was only weeks away from achieving her dream of entering a competition. That is how life is. Sometimes you are almost at the point of living your dreams and achieving your goals and then there are circumstances beyond your control, which set you back. Although Nina has been set back, she has not lost sight of her dream and may one day work her way back into competition form.

Setbacks may come and your dreams may be deferred. Do not give up and do not allow your dreams to die.

CHAPTER 18

Another Dream

When our older son, Mychal-David, was in the first grade, he loved drawing stick people. In fact, he loved drawing stick people so much that he often did not do any other schoolwork. Not only that, he was constantly in trouble at school about one thing or another. Sound familiar? We were always getting calls from the school.

"Mychal-David hit a little boy."

"Mychal-David hit a little boy."

"Mychal-David pushed a little boy at PE."

If we were not getting telephone calls we were getting notes from his teachers.

"Mychal-David was throwing popcorn in music class."

"Mychal-David wouldn't follow instructions."

My wife and I enrolled him in Ho Shin Do Karate to help him to develop discipline and to better manage his behavior. We also enrolled him in after-school art classes and in art camp between first and second grades. We discovered that our son had a passion for art, in the same way in which I had a passion for writing poetry in the second grade, and in the same way in which Nina had a passion for sports.

Eventually, he began to develop his own dreams of becoming an artist. With each art class, he was becoming better and better. His schoolwork was getting better and the karate classes were helping him to better manage his behavior.

My wife and I knew that the school where he was going was a good school, but taking art one day a week for 30 minutes would not help him develop his passion and was not enough to help him to develop his dream. We could not run our company for only 30 minutes a week and expect to be successful. I could not write for only 30 minutes a week and expect to be successful. Nina could not work out for only 30 minutes a week and expect to reach her dream of competing.

As I went to the library to expand my knowledge of writing and publishing, as Nina went each day to the health club and to a personal trainer to develop her body for competition, we began looking for a public school where our son could expand his knowledge and develop his artistic talents. We looked at schools in Charleston, South Carolina; Fort Myers, Florida; and St. Petersburg, Florida. As in the pursuit of any dream, you need a plan. When Mychal-David was in the fourth grade, during Spring Break, we took a family trip from Atlanta, Georgia, to Charleston, South Carolina, to Fort Myers, Florida, and to St. Petersburg, Florida. We looked at all three schools and my wife and I considered all three cities. We finally decided the best of the three cities for us to relocate our business and our family was the St. Petersburg/Tampa/Clearwater, Florida, area. Not only did it require us to relocate our family and our company, we had to buy a house in the neighborhood near the school.

It was time for another plan. So that our son could attend Perkins Elementary Magnet School of the Arts, to continue following his dream to become an artist, we had to move from our 6 bedroom, 4 bathroom, 5,500 square foot home into a 2 bedroom, 1 bathroom, 672 square foot home!

Nina and I really had to talk about this one. Her dreams of competing in a bodybuilding competition would have to be put on hold again. We would have to move our entire publishing company from Marietta, Georgia, to St. Petersburg, Florida, so that this ten-year-old kid could have an opportunity to further develop his talent to pursue his dream.

Most of our friends and all of Nina's family thought that we had both lost our minds. Why not simply let this kid continue taking art classes after school and go to art camp in the summer? What was the big deal?

I guess the big deal was me. Nina's a lot smarter than I am. The closer the time came for packing our things and moving to this tiny little house in Florida, the more she began thinking that perhaps my illness during the time that I was in the hospital had somehow affected more than just my heart. It must have also affected my brain!

This was another situation that required courage. Most of our friends thought we were crazy (you are probably thinking we were crazy also). I was at a school sharing this story with students and a young lady in the seventh grade raised her hand. "Mr. Wynn, you mean that you moved out of the big house to that tiny little house just so your son could attend this art school? I'm sorry Mr. Wynn, but I agree with your friends. I don't mean any disrespect, but you must have been crazy!"

What other people think or say has never bothered me since that young lady at Venice Beach who did not think my poetry was worth two dollars. The only person who really mattered was Nina. Nina married me and in her vows she stood before God and witnesses and said, "For better, for worse, for richer, for poorer, in sickness, and in health, 'til death do us part." Those vows were important to her, so she packed our bags and we were off to Florida.

We lived in St. Petersburg, Florida, for three years. During that time, our older son, Mychal-David, became an extraordinary artist and illustrator.

After relocating back to Georgia, he continued pursuing art through the Visual/Performing Arts and Math/Science Magnet Programs at North Springs High School in Atlanta, Georgia. He played football, ran track, and played lacrosse. As a result of his extracurricular activities, academic achievements, and art portfolio, he was accepted in first-choice college, Amherst College, located in Amherst, Massachusetts. While he is still expanding his illustrative and computer animation skills, his dreams have continued to expand as he considers law school and possibly politics.

Our younger son, Jalani, is now attending middle school and wants to attend the Ivy League school of Yale, one of the country's top-ranked major universities. We suspect that hidden within Jalani's academic, acting, singing, writing, and athletic abilities are dreams, which today, are still unimaginable.

You never know where your dreams will take you.

CHAPTER 19

What About Your Dreams?

I have shared my story because I want to inspire you to discover your dreams. Whatever your circumstances, whatever your situation, whatever your obstacles, I wanted you to hear the story of someone who started out with obstacles and circumstances that could have easily caused him to quit.

Your situation may be more difficult than mine. You may have more obstacles than I did. You may not even have a dream like I did. However, I want you to think. No one else can think for you. You must think for yourself and I have a list of questions I would like for you to think about.

1. *What do you like to do?*
2. *What types of things are you really good at?*
3. *What would you do for the rest of your life, even if you did not get paid for doing it?*
4. *What are some of the careers related to your interests, and that utilize your skills?*
5. *What classes, programs, camps, or clubs are available at your school or within your community, which can help you to develop the talents, skills, abilities, experiences, and knowledge needed to follow your dreams?*

After you have given careful thought to these five questions, I have five more things I would like to encourage you to do:

1. *Find someone who has already succeeded at what you are interested in doing and ask them for advice.*
2. *Read, read, read. Become an expert in the areas of your dreams.*
3. *Whenever possible, take classes in school that relate to your dreams.*
4. *Identify at least three colleges where you could pursue your dreams.*
5. *Identify what you must do to be accepted into each of the three colleges that you have identified.*

If you identified eating as one of the things you like to do, then your "real dream" may be to own a restaurant or to become a chef!

If you identified working on cars as one of the things you like to do, then your real dream may be to race, sell, design, test drive or write about automobiles.

If you identified playing a sport or physical fitness as one of the things you like to do, then your real dream may be to become a personal trainer, physical fitness spokesperson, own a health food store, start a health and fitness company, compete in a bodybuilding competition, become a sports agent, or become a doctor specializing in sports medicine.

If you identified talking to people, figuring things out or helping others, then your real dream may be to become a teacher.

The point is, if you can identify your real dream, then you can use the time while you are in school to *research*, write about, *research*, talk about, *research*, illustrate, *research*, create projects, *research*, identify places to go, *research*, identify trade associations, *research*, identify related extracurricular activities, *research*, identify schools that specialize in your areas of interest, *research*, identify books or people who are knowledgeable about your areas of interest, *research,* or ask a teacher to help you.

Whenever we talk about dreams, we typically think of jobs or careers. Try to think about your dreams as the things you would like to do, the things you would like to change, the places you would like to go or the type of family and community you would like to have. Any of these things could lead to the job or career that you need to support you and your family. Keep in mind that writing was my dream and getting paid for what I write has become my career. Having a wife, children, a home, and helping other people were all parts of my dream.

There are several things you can do to begin focusing on your dreams. Try writing about all of the important things in your life today and the types of things you feel would be important to have or to be involved in, in the future. For example, is family important to you? Is your church or your faith important to you? Would owning your own business or having a certain type of job or career be important to you? Are there political issues, environmental concerns or social changes you want to become involved in?

Gather together some magazines that reflect the things that are important to you; for example, sports magazines, entertainment magazines, career or business magazines, etc. Cut out pictures and words that reflect the things which are important to you or which you would like to achieve in the future. This may include images of people, cars, homes, etc. Get a piece of poster board and glue all of the words and images onto the poster board. Place this board onto a wall where you can look at it every day. Use this "Dream Board" to stay focused on your dreams.

Talk to as many people as you can, to develop the best plan you can, to help you to focus on the types of things you need to do to achieve your dreams. Usually, we achieve our dreams step-by-step and one-by-one, not all at once. Learn how to be patient. My passion for writing began when I was seven years old. However, I did not publish my first book until I was thirty-two years old. I have now written and published over twenty books and I have many, many other dreams—enough to keep me busy for the rest of my life.

Hopefully, reading this book has inspired you to think about your own dreams. If you are currently attending elementary, middle, or high school, you must begin thinking about, "What will I do after high school?" Answering this question will assist you in avoiding some of the poor choices that I made during my years in elementary, middle, and high school.

No matter what your dreams are, you must have a plan. For most dreams, that plan will include college. To assist you with your college-bound plans I have written a college-planning series of books and workbooks.

On the following page is one of the poems from my book of poetry, *Don't Quit*, a poem, which I believe, captures the spirit of all that I have done. As you read the words, be encouraged. No matter how great your journey or how rough your road, *There's A New Day Coming.*

There's A New Day Coming

When the Sun announces
.....the dawning day,
Just flex your muscles
.....and start on your way.
Go over or under,
.....around or through
Any obstacles or hurdles
.....that challenge you.
There's a new day coming.

Cast aside the failures
.....of yesterday,
Forget the peaks and valleys
.....that have paved your way.
Wipe the sweat from your brow
.....and the dust from your shoe,
Take a breath and relax
.....so that you may begin anew.
There's a new day coming.

Forget the burdens and obstacles
.....that have held you back,
Focus on your dreams
.....and prepare a plan of attack.
There are battles awaiting
.....to challenge your success,

Daring you to stand tall
    and to give it your best.
There's a new day coming.

No matter how great the journey,
    or how heavy the load,
How steep the mountain
    or how rough the road.
When your arms grow weary
    and legs give way,
Stop and rest for a moment
    it will be okay.
There's a new day coming.

As shadows spring forth
    from the setting Sun,
Take a moment and savor
    the battles you've won.
Sleep peacefully tonight
    and enjoy your rest,
Awaken tomorrow
    and continue your quest.
There's always, a new day coming.

– Mychal Wynn

Follow YOUR Dreams!

WHAT ARE YOUR GOALS?

Following your dreams will require that you begin setting goals. Take a moment to reflect on your dreams and use the following pages to write down some of your goals for the coming school year.

Some of the areas within which you may consider setting goals are:

- *Academic*
- *Athletic*
- *Creative (e.g., Art, Music, Dance, Drama, etc.)*
- *Personal Development*
- *Stronger Relationships with Family and Friends*
- *Community Service*
- *Clubs, Activities, Competitions*
- *Learning a Foreign Language*
- *Learning a New Skill*

Goals:

_____

_____

_____

_____

_____

_____

_____

_____

_____

_____

_____

_____

_____

_____

Goals:

_____

_____

_____

_____

_____

_____

_____

_____

_____

_____

_____

_____

_____

_____

_____

Goals:

_____

_____

_____

_____

_____

_____

_____

_____

_____

_____

_____

_____

_____

_____

Goals:

_____

_____

_____

_____

_____

_____

_____

_____

_____

_____

_____

_____

_____

Goals:

_____

_____

_____

_____

_____

_____

_____

_____

_____

_____

_____

_____

_____

_____

_____

_____

Goals:

_____

_____

_____

_____

_____

_____

_____

_____

_____

_____

_____

_____

_____

_____

_____

Goals:

_____

_____

_____

_____

_____

_____

_____

_____

_____

_____

_____

_____

_____

_____

Goals:

_____

_____

_____

_____

_____

_____

_____

_____

_____

_____

_____

_____

_____

_____

_____

_____

Goals:

_____

_____

_____

_____

_____

_____

_____

_____

_____

_____

_____

_____

_____

Goals:

_____

_____

_____

_____

_____

_____

_____

_____

_____

_____

_____

_____

_____

_____

_____

Goals:

_____

_____

_____

_____

_____

_____

_____

_____

_____

_____

_____

_____

_____

_____

_____

_____

– Other books by Mychal Wynn –

A High School Plan for Students with College-Bound Dreams

Quick Guide (ISBN 1-880463-68-7 • $5.95)
Book (ISBN 1-880463-66-0 • $19.95)
Workbook (ISBN 1-880463-80-6 • $15.95)

Easy-to-follow planning guides to assist in developing 4-year high school plans. Explains how grades, standardized tests, behavior, activities, classes, community service, essays, and teacher recommendations can all be factored into a plan that can prepare students for, and be accepted into, their first-choice college(s).

A Middle School Plan for Students with College-Bound Dreams

Quick Guide (ISBN 1-880463-05-9 • $5.95)
Book (ISBN 1-880463-67-9 • $15.95)
Workbook (ISBN 1-880463-00-8 • $15.95)

Easy-to-follow planning guides to assist in developing 3-year middle school plans. Explores learning styles, personality types, best and worst learning situations as they outline how to maximize the middle school experience as part of a 7-year middle-through-high school plan.

Don't Quit (ISBN 1-880463-26-1 • $9.95)

Mychal Wynn's critically-acclaimed book of poetry contains 26 poems of inspiration and affirmation. Each verse is complemented by an inspiring quotation.

Ten Steps to Helping Your Child Succeed in School
(ISBN 1-880463-50-4 • $9.95)

Outlines easy-to-follow steps for parents and teachers to better understand children so that we can better direct them. The steps help parents and teachers to easily identify a child's personality types, learning styles, Multiple Intelligences, best and worst learning situations, dreams and aspirations.

Test of Faith: A Personal Testimony of God's Grace,
Mercy, and Omnipotent Power
(ISBN 1-880463-09-1 • $9.95)

"This book has become more than a recalling of my hospital experiences, it has become a testimony of the power of the human spirit; a testimony of the healing power of the Holy Spirit; and ultimately a personal testimony of my relationship with God, my belief in His anointing, and my trust in His power, grace, and mercy."

The Eagles who Thought They were Chickens: A Tale of Discovery

Book (ISBN 1-880463-12-1 • $4.95)
Student Activity Book (ISBN 1-880463-19-9 • $5.95)
Teacher's Guide (ISBN 1 880463-18-0 • $9.95)

Chronicles the journey of a great eagle, historically perched at the right hand of the great king in her native Africa, who is captured and taken aboard a slave ship, the eggs that are eventually hatched, and their struggles in the chicken yard where they are scorned and ridiculed for their differences. The story offers parallels to behaviors in classrooms and on school playgrounds where children are teased by schoolyard "chickens" and bullied by schoolyard "roosters."

To correspond with Mr. Wynn, write to:

Mychal Wynn
c/o Rising Sun Publishing
P.O. Box 70906
Marietta, GA 30007

To order additional copies of this, or other books by Mr. Wynn, visit our web site:

www.rspublishing.com

Send your email to:

info@rspublishing.com